W9-CYE-140

FAN FEAST!

The NY Giants Fan Guide to Tailgating

Willie "The Pizza Man" Mariano

TRIUMPH
BOOKS
CHICAGO

First and foremost I thank God for giving me the gift of life and the courage to live it. I also thank my fellow coworkers at the Big Blue Travel for all their support and encouragement, especially Michael Martocci and Barry Liben. To my packagers Linda and Peter Kosarin and John Rutledge, we made it! Who'da thunk it? To Rusty Hawley, Doug Murphy, and the rest of the New York Football Giants family, thanks for all your help and for believing in me. To anyone who I may have forgotten, thank you. Last but not least, thank you to all those faithful Giants fans for making going to Giants Stadium a family affair.

Contents

From the Sea

Pass the Pasta!

Gumbos, Stews, Chilis, & Sauces

Snacks & Sides

Dedication

The only way I can truly explain how I finally got this Nobel Prize-worthy book on the shelves is to tell you about the wonderful people in my life. The first are my parents, Grace and Tony, or as we fondly call them, "K. C. and Gordie," the biggest Giants fans in the world. Without you inspiring me in the art of tailgating, this book never could have been written. You taught me never to quit. You are the best people I know, the greatest parents a man can ask for, and I love you with all my heart. To my brother Tony and my sister Teresa, thanks for being there when I needed you most.

To my friend, lover, and soulmate, Mary, I could not have done this without you. You had a vision and helped me see it. Your belief in me and your neverending love is what got me here. You also have given me the gift of fatherhood. For all this I thank you. To my three beautiful Pizza Girls, Gabrielle, Angelica, and Christiana, you are the reason I wake up every day. Always remember daddy is only a wish or a dream away, no matter what. I love you! When I am far away, all you need to do is close your eyes and daddy will be right there to guide you to wherever your dreams want to go.

To the Giants players, coaches, and staff who have come to know me, I thank you for all your encouragement and kind words, but most of all for being Giants.

To those who know me, those who know of me, and those who will come to know me, thank you for your support and generosity. I hope that each of you have at least one of your dreams come true.

To my angel, who exists in my mind and soul, and has helped me through the trying times, thank you for helping me spread my wings.

Last, but not least, are the two men in my life that helped make all this possible, Michael Martocci and Barry Liben. This book would not have been possible if it were not for your belief in my ability. Michael, I thank you for giving me the chance to show my dedication to you and Big Blue Travel, the one and only Official Road Trip Company of our New York Football Giants. You have my neverending friendship, "Grazie mille, mio amico bella."

To Barry Liben, the owner of one of the largest travel companies in the world, Tzell Travel, "The Big Boss Man " behind the "Big Desk," you showed me in one short twenty-minute meeting the special person that I always knew you were. You have welcomed me as family and for this you have my loyalty and friendship in return. To "Le Grande Formaggio" I simply say thank you for your faith and trust in me. It will never be unwarranted.

Giant Beginnings

Photo by Seth Dinnerman

Photo by Linda Kosarin

Photo by Al Pereira

The Roaring Twenties

The 1920s . . . America's industrial heartbeat was loud and strong. The war to end all wars was beginning to take its place as a chapter in our evolving history. The Charleston and the Black Bottom were all the rage, and flappers scandalized a country that was on the verge of redefining its cultural values.

The Volstead Act, adopted in 1919, prohibited the manufacture, sale, and possession of alcoholic beverages. While it was the law of the land, Americans continued to deliver "backhand slaps" to both the lawmakers and those who tried to enforce it. Homemade bathtub gin as well as "speakeasies," private clubs for the illegal purchase and consumption of alcohol, were available in practically any neighborhood. America's thirst for alcohol also helped spawn a major growth in organized crime. Al Capone, Bugsy Siegel, the Saint Valentine's Day Massacre, and the headline-grabbing gang wars and multiple murders would become bookmarks of infamy during this turbulent decade.

The energy and enthusiasm of a country on the verge of claiming prominence as a world leader was not lost on its citizens. The economy was strong, the future was bright, and America was beginning to flex its cultural muscle. Tastes in clothes, music, theater, and lifestyles were changing rapidly. It is often said that a country can be understood most easily by how its people recreate. In America during the 1920s and 1930s, sports was king.

Baseball, bike racing at velodromes throughout the country, racewalking, boxing, tennis, and other sports were all the rage. Americans wanted still more. In small factory towns throughout America, makeshift teams of worker-athletes were beginning to lay the foundation for a sport that would someday challenge rival baseball's title as America's favorite pastime.

Teams with names like the Rochester Jeffersons, Canton Bulldogs, Providence Steam Roller, Kenosha Maroons, and the Racine Legion struggled to find their place in a newly

Giants Historical Highlights— Championships:

Super Bowl Championships:
XXI, 1987
XXV, 1991

NFL Championships:
1927, 1934, 1938, 1956

NFC Championships:
1986, 1990

3

formed group called the National Football League. Many of the teams were facing financial hard times because the small towns in which they were located had difficulty generating enough fan support to make the teams profitable. However, the league persisted and ultimately grew to what it is today.

In 1925, Tim Mara, a successful sports bookmaker (gambling was legal at the time) paid $500 to acquire the National Football League (NFL) franchise for a New York football team. Mara, who conducted his business at New York racetracks under a striped umbrella, was heard later to remark, "A franchise for anything in New York is worth $500, including shining shoes."

His franchise, the New York Football Giants, has been one of the cornerstones of the NFL. Blessed with the most knowledgeable, loyal, and passionate fans in all of sports, the New York Football Giants remain one of the elite team franchises.

So, loyal and true-blue Giants fans, it is with a sense of history and a greater sense of future that this humble work is dedicated to you, the heart and soul and the best twelfth man any team could ever hope for.

Go Giants!

Willie "The Pizza Man" Mariano

A Brief History of the New York Giants

After his purchase of the New York football franchise in 1925, Tim Mara and his contemporaries, men like Art Rooney, Bert Bell, George Preston Marshall, and Earl (Curly) Lambeau, would help establish the foundation on which the NFL was built.

After purchasing the franchise, Mara negotiated for the team to play at the Polo Grounds, the home of the New York Baseball Giants. Recognizing that baseball was the national pastime and football was the upstart new kid on the block, Mara decided to name the team the New York Football Giants in the hope of capitalizing on the name recognition of the baseball team.

During its first decade, the team struggled financially even though they won their first of many championships in just their third season. During the depression era, when the economy plummeted and the market crashed, Tim Mara decided to relinquish control of the team to his two sons, twenty-two-year-old Jack and fourteen-year-old Wellington. Wellington was not only beginning a long and storied career with the Giants, he was also the youngest person in National Football League history to own a professional team.

In 1934, the Giants won their second championship in what has gone down in history as the "sneakers game."

With the temperatures near zero and the Polo Grounds field icy, the Giants seemed destined to lose their second championship game in a row. Trailing the rival Chicago Bears 13–3 at halftime, with conditions continuing to deteriorate, the Giants needed all the help they could get. "Stout" Steve Owen, the Giants' quick-thinking head coach, realized that his players' cleats were useless on the frozen turf.

Realizing that one of his assistants was also the basketball coach at Columbia University, Owen dispatched him in a taxi to Columbia to borrow the basketball team's sneakers.

NFL Eastern Conference Championships:
1933, 1934, 1935, 1938, 1939, 1941, 1944, 1946, 1956, 1958, 1959, 1961, 1962, 1963

NFC Eastern Division Championships:
1986, 1989, 1990, 1997

Jersey Numbering System

In 1949, the league allowed pass receivers to wear different colored helmets from the rest of the team, so a quarterback could recognize his receivers. This was one of the first steps toward a standard jersey numbering system.

The Cleveland Browns started assigning jersey numbers to positions while in the All-America Football Conference in the late 1940s. In 1952, the NFL established the system of jersey numbers used today. The different-colored helmets option was eliminated in 1973, and from that point on no exceptions to the jersey rule were allowed.

Owen's quick thinking paid off. The Giants, wearing the borrowed sneakers, went on to beat the Bears and win the championship with a twenty-seven-point fourth quarter.

After the Giants won their third NFL championship by beating the Green Bay Packers in 1938, and then losing the championship to the Packers the very next year, came the difficult 1940s. It was a decade of survival not just for the Giants and the rest of the NFL, but for America as well. World War II was raging, and the league was in danger of folding. While losing the majority of their players to military service, the Giants, like the country and the NFL, managed to persevere, and they played in three championship games during the decade.

The 1950s brought some of the most prominent names in Giants history: Kyle Rote, Rosey Brown, Sam Huff, Frank Gifford, Dick Lynch, and Tom Landry, just to name a few.

The team remained prominent until the early years of the 1960s when they managed to lose three straight title games with one crushing defeat after another. The existing team was aging rapidly and injuries to key players came in alarming numbers. Fans could not wait to put the sixties behind them and get on with the future. Unfortunately, the Giants would continue through the seventies as a team in transition, playing in three different states and four different stadiums and finishing last or next to last eight out of ten times.

Finally, the Giants reached the 1980s, and what a decade it would become for long-suffering Giants fans. We were treated to the exploits of perhaps the best defensive player the game has ever seen: No. 56, Lawrence Taylor. Additionally, players such as Jim Burt, Harry Carson, Mark Bavaro, and of course Phil Simms were at the zenith of their careers and helped deliver two Super Bowl wins in the process. While there were numerous coaching and player changes during the early 1990s and the team seemed to take a few steps backward, new head coach Jim Fassel appears to be on the verge of bringing the glory days back to Giants Stadium. Once again the chant of "Go Big Blue" echoes throughout the parking lots at the Meadowlands as the tailgaters feast before the games.

New York Giants Administrative, Coaching, and Player Personnel Staffs

In 1979, centers were included as interior linemen in numbering positions.

Over the last several years, teams have expanded the number of wide receivers, H-backs, and tight ends, and occasionally have run out of numbers for these players.

Because of the need for additional numbers, in 1995 the league permitted receivers to wear numbers from 10 to 19.

Administrative Officers

- Wellington Mara—President /co-CEO
- Preston R. Tisch—Chairman /co-CEO
- John K. Mara—Executive VP/General Counsel
- Jonathan M. Tisch—Treasurer
- Ernie Accorsi—VP/General Manager
- John Pasquali—VP/CFO
- Pat Hanlon—VP Public Relations
- Rusty Hawley—VP Marketing

Front Office Executives

- Jim Phelan—Director of Administration
- John Gorman—Ticket Manager
- Francis X. Mara—Director of Promotions
- Christine Procops—Controller
- Avis Roper—Asst. Director Public Relations
- Dan Lynch—Director of Sales
- William Smith—Asst. Director Marketing
- Doug Murphy—Director of Creative Services
- Allison Stangeby—Director of Community Relations

Player Personnel

- Rich Donohue—Asst. General Manager
- Tom Boisture—VP Player Personnel
- Marv Sunderland—Director Player Personnel
- Jerry Shay—Director College Scouting
- David Gettleman—Director Pro Personnel

The following are the group numbers assigned to players at different positions:

Quarterbacks, placekickers, and punters: 1 to 19.

Running backs and defensive backs: 20 to 49.

- Raymond J. Walsh, Jr.—Director R&D
- John Berger—Director Computer Services
- Tony Ceglio—Director Video Operations
- John Mancuso—Video Director
- Dave Maltese—Asst. Video Director

Coaches

- Jim Fassel—Head Coach
- John Fox—Defensive Coordinator
- Jim Skipper—Offensive Coordinator/Running Backs

Assistant Coaches

- Denny Marcin—Defensive Line
- Jimmy Robinson—Wide Receivers
- John Dunn—Strength/Conditioning
- Craig Stoddard—Asst. Strength/Conditioning
- Jim McNally—Offensive Line
- Larry MacDuff—Special Teams
- Mike Haluchak—Linebackers
- Johnnie Lynn—Defensive Backs
- Dick Rehbein—Tight Ends
- Dave Brazil—Defensive Quality Control
- Mike Gillhamer—Offensive Quality Control
- Sean Payton—Quarterback Coach

Team Physician and Staff

- Dr. Russell F. Warren—Team Physician
- Dr. Allan Levy—Associate Team Physician
- Dr. Stephen J. O'Brien—Associate Team Physician
- Dr. Joel Goldberg—Director of Career Counseling
- Dr. Hugh Gardy—Team Dentist
- Heidi Skolnik—Nutrition Consultant

Athletic Trainers

- Ronnie Barnes—Head Athletic Trainer
- Steve Kennelly—Athletic Trainer
- Byron Hansen—Athletic Trainer
- John Johnson—Athletic Trainer

Equipment Handlers

- Ed Wagner—Locker Room Manager
- Ed Wagner Jr.—Equipment Manager
- Jim Phelan—Assistant
- Joe Skiba—Assistant
- Ed Skiba—Assistant
- Joe Mansfield—Field Security Manager
- Julius Horai—Administrative Assistant

Scouting Staff

- Rosey Brown—Scout
- John Crea—Scout
- Jeremiah Davis—Scout
- Greg Gabriel—Scout
- Ken Kavanaugh—Scout
- Jerry Reese—Scout
- Steve Verderosa—Scout

Centers: 50 to 59 (60 to 79 if those numbers are unavailable).

Linebackers: 50 to 59 (90 to 99 if numbers are unavailable).

Offensive guards and tackles: 60 to 79.

Wide receivers and tight ends: 80 to 89 (10 to 19 if those numbers are unavailable).

Defensive linemen: 60 to 79 (90 to 99 if those numbers are unavailable).

Giants Ticket Information

Season tickets for the Giants are always sold out. While you can request to be put on the very long waiting list, your chances of obtaining a season ticket through conventional means is almost impossible. Send your ticket requests to:

Ticket Department
New York Football Giants
Giants Stadium
East Rutherford, NJ 07073

Ticket information phone numbers:
General Box Office (201) 935-3900
Group Ticket Sales (201) 460-4370

Big Blue Travel, the official road-trip company for the Giants, offers tour packages for most of the Giants away games. Contact them at: (212) 944-2121.

Additional phone numbers of interest to Giants fans:

New York Football Giants, Inc.
East Rutherford, NJ 07073
(201) 935-8111

National Football League
280 Park Ave.
New York, NY 10017
(212) 450-2000

NFL Players Association
2021 L Street NW, Suite 600
Washington, DC 20036
(202) 463-2200

NFL Properties, Inc.
(212) 838-0660 New York
(310) 215-1606 Los Angeles

Pro Football Hall of Fame
2121 George Halas Drive NW
Canton, Ohio 44708
(330) 456-8207

NFL Catalog ($1 charge)
10812 Alder Circle, Suite 5984
Dallas, Texas 75238

NFL Punt, Pass and Kick Information
1-800-NFL-SNAP

If a player wears a jersey that is not assigned to a position and walks onto the field, his team is penalized five yards and a loss of a down. This is considered an "illegal equipment" penalty.

**Pizza Man's
Fun Football Stuff**

Historical Firsts

**Football's Origins in
the U.S.:** Sport his-
torians generally
agree that the first
football game in the
U.S. took place on
November 6, 1869,
between Rutgers
and Princeton
Universities. Each
team used twenty-
five players at a
time.

Giants Meadowlands Stadium Facts

Meadowlands Sports Complex: *The Meadowlands Sports Complex, which consists of Giants Stadium, Continental Airlines Arena, and the Meadowlands Racetrack, occupies a 750-acre site in East Rutherford, New Jersey. The complex cost $450 million and is recognized as one of the great sports and entertainment complexes in the world.*

Groundbreaking: *November 19, 1972*

Capacity: *77,716 (football); 55,000 to 60,000 (concerts)*

Opening Day: *October 10, 1976. A sold-out crowd of 76,042 watched the Dallas Cowboys defeat the Giants 24–14.*

Specifications: *Length: 756 feet, width: 592 feet, height: 144 feet*

Concrete & Steel: *13,500 tons (27,000,000 pounds) of structural steel and 29,200 cubic yards of poured concrete.*

Roof Type: *Open*

Cost: *$75 million*

Site Size: *20.25 acres*

Available Parking: *25,000 parking spaces*

Playing Surface: *Astroturf (football); grass (soccer)*

Management: *New Jersey Sports and Exposition Authority*

Tenants: *Giants and Jets (NFL); Metro Stars (MLS)*

Luxury Suites: *118–72 on mezzanine level: 70 suites seat 16, 2 suites seat 10; 26 new Tower suites seat 16; 6 Super suites seat 16 or 22; 14 Terrace suites seat 20. Yearly prices for these luxury suites range from $125,000 to $350,000, depending on location.*

Stadium Concessionaire: *ARAMARK, INC.*

Concession Stands: *40 concession stands, 70 carts*

Restaurant: *Stadium Club is located on ground floor. Dining room and bar covers 14,540 square feet and has a capacity of 2,000.*

Press Box: *Upper press box has 300 workstations with an adjoining lounge and dining room that seats 125. Located on the 50-yard line. Lower level press box has 16 individual booths for TV and radio broadcasters, cameras, coaches, scoreboard operator, and public address announcer.*

Video Boards: *Two Sony Jumbotron color video scoreboards in each end zone. Scoreboards measure 32 feet by 24 feet and are supported by two Daktronics Matrix black-and-white scoreboards plus four auxiliary scoreboards.*

Public Address System: *System generates over 27,000 audible watts utilizing 2,100 speakers and more than 47 miles of wiring cable.*

Field Lighting: *576 metal halide lamps, 1,500 watts each.*

Restrooms: *35 Men's, 35 Women's*

Ticket Windows: *50*

All-Time Attendance Record: *82,948 on October 5, 1995, for a mass celebrated by Pope John Paul II.*

Photo by Linda Kosarin

13

Giants Stadium

Gate B Access To All Levels

Gate C Access To All Levels

Gate A Access To All Levels

Gate D Access To All Levels

Press Box

Higher numbered seat is closer to higher numbered section

Mens Room
Womens Room
Physically Challenged

First Aid
Concessions
Telephone

Giants Stadium East Rutherford, NJ 07073

GIANTS STADIUM

Giants Stadium Tailgating Regulations

Tailgating allowed? *Yes*

Designated tailgating lots? *No*

Can you reserve spaces? *No*

Parking costs for cars or RVs? *$10*

Separate area for RVs? *No*

When are lots open? *Four and a half hours before kickoff*

Overnight parking? *No*

Tents allowed? *No*

Charcoal or gas grills allowed? *Yes*

Alcohol allowed? *Yes, but no kegs*

Used-charcoal disposal sites? *No*

Bathroom facilities? *Yes, portable*

First Pro Football Game: The first professional football game in the U.S. took place at Latrobe, Pennsylvania, between a team from Latrobe and a team from Jeannette, Pennsylvania. The first professional league, the American Professional Football Association, was formed in 1920. In 1922, the AMPFA gave way to the newly-formed NFL.

On the Road with Big Blue

Being on the road with Big Blue Travel has been a dream come true for me. Here I am, an average guy from Bensonhurst, traveling to all the away games with my beloved team. I get to stay in five-star hotels across the country, eat at all the finest restaurants each city has to offer, hang with players from the New York Football Giants, and best of all, I get to go to the unfriendly confines of the opposing team's stadium. I get to voice my infamous words of discouragement to the opposing team, in their own stadium.

You might say, "You must be out of your mind. Why would anyone like going to a stadium with seventy thousand fans in a city where you are not welcome?" The grief I get usually starts in the parking lot as I am walking to the stadium. Could it be because I'm dressed in Giants colors, from my trademark Giants hard hat to my "Pizza Man" jersey? It doesn't really matter what city I am in, the words of "endearment" from the opposing fans are all the same. No matter where I am, I wear my Giants colors with pride. You see, people who know me understand I'm not the type to take the verbal abuse that is shouted at me. Not this Pizza Dude. I go right back at them with the verve and conviction that was taught to me by my mom.

That's right, I did say my mom. This is a woman who not only successfully raised three children, but is the biggest sports fan I know. She not only is the best mom in the world, she is the biggest Giants fan there is. The hardest part of moving to Florida eight years ago was not that she was going to miss her children and grandchildren, but that she had to give up her season tickets for the Giants. It was just as hard for my dad, I'm sure, but Mom was really going through withdrawal for the first few years. Much to Mom's dismay, the community they lived in did not allow satellite dishes. Religiously, for the first three

Photo by Mike Malarkey

16

years they lived there, Mom would make my dad drive three hours to Tampa from Fort Myers to a sports bar every Sunday to watch "Her Giants."

After my dad couldn't make the drive anymore because of his health, they did the only thing they could do—they moved to a community that allowed satellite dishes and purchased the biggest one they could find. I guess what they say is true: "The apple doesn't fall far from the tree."

This is why I do what I do. It's part of my gene pool. It's the reason why I like to go into the stadium an hour or so before kickoff and voice my opinions to the opposing players. Remember, I do this without using any profanity, while making sure I maintain the dignity and class the Giants organization deserves. Unfortunately, I cannot say that for the other teams' fans. There are a few exceptions, but not many.

While in Washington for the first time in 1996, I happened to be sitting in the same section as Zema "Chief Zee" Williams. Here is a guy that anyone who has been watching football over the years has come to recognize. He is a D.C. legend who is always dressed as an Indian chief, complete with head-dress. You've seen him on television many times. There I was, sitting in RFK Stadium rooting for my Giants, when he got up and walked over to me. I really thought I was going to be harassed by "Chief Zee," but I could not have been more wrong. He walked up to me, extended his hand in friendship, and said, "You're that 'Pizza' dude I always see on the high-light films, aren't you?"

I stood there in shock, unable to speak. I know the people who know me will say this is impossible, but it's true. Here is a guy I grew up watching root for his team, seemingly never missing a game, and he wanted to shake my hand, to tell me I'm known to him because I do for my team what he does for his. This to me is what the great game of NFL foot-ball is all about, sticking by your team no matter what and having fun while doing it. The camaraderie we shared that night will always be special to me. Then again, he's a Redskins fan, so he should have been honored to shake a Giants fan's hand, right?

Giants' First Home Field: New York's Polo Grounds, home to the Baseball Giants, 1925–55.

Giants' First Regular Season Game: A 14–0 loss to Providence Steam Roller on October 11, 1925.

First Regular Season Win: A 19–0 victory over the Cleveland Bulldogs on November 1, 1925.

First Regular Season Points: A dropkicked fifteen-yard field goal by Matt Brennan in a 5–3 loss to the Frankford Yellow Jackets on October 17, 1925.

First Winning Season: 1925, when they went 8–4.

First Championship Season: 1927, when they went 11–1–1.

An Open Letter to Coach Fassel and Staff

On behalf of all Giants fans, I would like to say to our team, team owners, and coaching staff, that you have given all Giants fans a reason to look forward to football Sundays again. Thank you! You, like most New Yorkers, believe in hard work, staying true blue, and never quitting until the task at hand is complete. Once you get to the dance, you may as well try to take home the queen.

We're back. The New York Football Giants were the National Football Conference (NFC) Eastern Division Champions in '97!! Boy, I can read that headline all day long and not grow tired of it, but we all know what we really want to see on the front pages. Nineteen-ninety-eight was a disappointing year when we went only 8–8, due to some injuries and shakiness at quarterback. However, we always look to the future.

Dare we say Super Bowl? Our fine Coach of the Year doesn't seem to mind saying it. After all, he said, "By making the playoffs, the ultimate goal now is to win The Big One."

Wow! What a quote from a guy most fans knew nothing about. He was brought here as an offensive doctor to try and stop the bleeding of a team that had almost no blood left.

He has transplanted pride and tradition back into the hearts of all Giants faithful, molding a collection of no-name athletes into a team that plays as a unit with a hunger and determination parallel to those great Giants teams of the past. True fans fondly remember them.

Coach Fassel, you came here hailed as a quarterback guru, using an approach most of us use in our everyday lives as city dwellers—respect those who work for you and with you, while demanding only trust and belief that hard work will bring success.

You have accomplished this while brightening the future of upcoming seasons. I'm sure I reflect the feelings of all Giants fans when I say after years of rebuilding, we couldn't have dreamed of a better way to start your term as the boss. Thanks, Coach!!

GO BIG BLUE!!!

See you at the stadium.

Willie "The Pizza Man" Mariano

Photo by Mike Malarkey

The Art of Tailgating
"Pizza Man" Style

Photo by Seth Dinnerman

Photo by Seth Dinnerman

Photo by Linda Kosarin

How the "Pizza Man" Got His Name

Many of you might wonder how I came to be called the "Pizza Man." Some of you might assume that I own a pizza shop or flip pies for a living: good guess, but wrong answer.

Some of you believe it is from all the pizza I eat. While I will admit to eating pizza several times during the week, and fancy myself a pizza connoisseur, that's not the reason. (However, if you want to know where the best pizzerias are in Brooklyn, just contact the Pizza Man for a list.)

Well, folks, the real story involves the NFL and the Home Box Office show, "Inside the NFL." It was 1982 at the Meadowlands and the Giants were due to play their hated rivals the Philadelphia Eagles. As usual, I had hosted one of my Monster Tailgate parties, and then headed into the stadium an hour before game time to continue my game-day ritual.

My seats are close to the tunnel where the players come onto the field from the locker rooms, and it is a great vantage point from which to "communicate" with the players. An hour or so before each game both the home team and the visitors take the field for calisthenics and drills. This is when I do my thing. Standing there in my Giants jersey and my one-of-a-kind hand-painted hard hat signed by LT himself, I began to "converse" with the enemy Eagles as they stretched.

An important point to be made is that I do not condone profanity and never use it when I am "interacting" with the opposing team's players.

So, as I was saying, when the Eagles started to come onto the field, I began warming up with a couple of collective jabs at them. Things like, "There's no brotherly

Photo by Mike Malarkey

23

More Historical Facts

First Giants Draft Pick: Tackle Art Lewis from Ohio University, 1936.

First All-NFL Selection: End Red Badger and Guard Butch Gibson, 1931.

First Giant to Rush for 100 Yards in a Game: Harry Newman rushed for 108 yards against the Boston Redskins on October 18, 1933.

love here for you guys," or "We're gonna make you into cheesesteaks today!" As I said, just a warm-up.

It was at that moment that I spotted Anton Davis, which is not hard to do, as big as he is. Anton is also one heck of a football player.

"Yo! Anton," I yelled. "What's your favorite part of the day, breakfast, lunch, and dinner? You're no athlete, get off the field. As a matter of fact, you should go have another pizza. Maybe a big boy like you needs two pies. Better yet, go on a diet, try a salad bar!" Anton chuckled, shook his massive head, and waved as he took the field.

While this exchange was going on, I was not even aware that the whole thing was being taped by the camera crew for "Inside the NFL." The night the show aired, I got a bunch of calls from friends and family telling me I made the highlight reel when I was yelling at Anton to get another pizza. I was happy to have been on TV, but it wasn't that big of a deal, or so I thought.

At the next home game, I was at my appointed spot by the tunnel waiting for the opposing players to take the field when I heard a couple of young kids say to their dad, "Hey, Dad, that's the pizza dude guy we saw on TV last week!" Dad looked at me kind of sheepishly and said, "Hey, Pizza Man, can we get an autograph?" My buddies from my tailgating crew looked at one another and began laughing. After they picked themselves up from the floor, they began chanting, "Pizza Man, Pizza Man." The kids picked up the chant and before I knew it another group of fans were picking up on the chant.

From that day forward, yours truly became the "Pizza Man." Much to my surprise, it took only a game or two before opposing players began to look for me at the tunnel and call out my new name. It is a really good feeling to be acknowledged by the opposition as a good-natured fan they can have some pregame fun with. Sometimes though, after an exceptionally tough loss to my Giants, my newfound friends, on the way to their locker room, wave to the Pizza Man and tell him where he should stick his hard hat. Oh well, such is the price of being recognized and bringing a fan's passion to the game.

Feast Like a Beast

It seems as if everyone is writing cookbooks these days. The recipes are getting more and more complicated and are more frustrating than fun to prepare. Everyone is so concerned about heart-healthy and eat-right diets that the joy of eating has all but been overlooked. No fat, low fat, less fat—to me it seems so boring. I believe anything cooked to perfection and eaten in moderation is fine. My tailgate recipes are fun, easy to prepare, and taste fantastic. They, along with my fondest memories of being a football fan, are the perfect catalyst to start off your terrific "Monster Tailgate" parties.

While I appreciate and respect what the doctors say about your blood pressure, heart rate, or cholesterol level, just remember, you go around only once in life. If you're lucky enough to have season tickets and get to tailgate a minimum of ten times a year, or join friends at a tailgate party, or decide to tailgate in your backyard and watch the game on TV, I say to all of you, "Feast like a beast!"

Photo by Seth Dinnerman

Tradition

The very best part about tailgating, besides the food, is the familiarity of almost everyone in the parking lot. As Giants fans, we already are known as the most knowledgeable and loyal fans in football, and it shows. The loyalty and dedication shown by the same fans week in and week out is quite evident. Although the names may change, the joy of being a fan never does, and we Giants fans consider it an honor to carry on the traditions that our fathers and grandfathers have passed on to us. The fans of the new millennium, like our team today, are young and full of the energy needed to have successful seasons and Monster Tailgates for many years to come.

Photo by Seth Dinnerman

Relax—It's a Party

The most important thing I do at each of my Monster Tailgate parties is try to relax. After all, Sunday is a day of rest, right? After methodically preparing a feast fit for kings, we then chow down like the true-blue-collar workers that we are. It is only after every morsel has been consumed, except for the snack bag we pack for halftime, that we are ready to go into the stadium. When I go down by the tunnel the players use to come onto the field and greet the enemy of the day, it's just another ritual to make sure I pump up my beloved Giants and rip away the confidence of the opposing team. I take pride in the good-natured razzing of the other team's players before kickoff. I also feel that those fans who have heard some of my post-game comments to the same players and who join me in this ritual also take pride in knowing that what we do is good, clean fun and a part of the game that should live forever. As long as we keep it lighthearted and free of profanity, and try only to take the other team off their game, then who do we hurt?

Photo by Linda Kosarin

First Giant to Rush for 1,000 Yards in a Season: Ron Johnson, 1,027 yards in 1970.

First Giant to Pass 400+ Yards in a Game: Y. A. Tittle passed for 505 yards in a game against the Washington Redskins for a then-club record on October 28, 1962.

Most Yards Rushing, Career: Rodney Hampton, 5,989 yards in 1990–95.

The Team Was Bad but Life Was Good

Growing up when I did in the seventies and eighties, there were many changes going on in the world. Except, of course, for our beloved "Big Blue." Unfortunately, they just stayed the same. Struggling from week to week, loss after loss, it looked as if nothing would ever change. Of course, being a true "Football Sunday Worshiper" like myself, you know that never mattered.

The way I looked at it in the early seventies was, I was alive, I was too young for Vietnam, and my parents were season-ticket holders for the New York Football Giants. Could life be any better? It was a charmed life to say the least, and it never mattered how bad the weather or our record was. Come Sunday in the fall and winter, we had Giants football. You might say I'm a nut, and you would be right. I'm nuts about the New York Football Giants.

Whether I was at my parent's house in Brooklyn or in a parking lot at Giants home games, there would always be great friends and family and even better food and drink. That, my fellow Giants fanatics, was the icing on the cake, the reason you worked hard all week while counting the minutes until the next "Football Sunday." What could possibly beat Mom's cooking and Dad's tailgating expertise? Not to mention their unwavering passion (passed down to me genetically) for Giants football. If you've ever had the honor of tasting any of their delectable delights, you would only say, "Incredible!" This, my friends, is my reason for writing this book, to share Mom and Dad's great dishes with the world. I hope that when you use these recipes, you too will feel the same as I do when sitting down to a real home-cooked meal. If you don't, then you're not cooking it right, and you should try again. Or you can always call my mom and dad. I am sure they will be happy to tell you how.

Confessions of a Football Fanatic

It has occurred to me that the only way for you to fully understand my passion for New York Giants football is to tell you what I go through from the minute a season ends until the beginning of a new one.

Whether it ends on the sixteenth week of the season or if my Giants are fortunate enough to make it all the way to the Ultimate Game, the Super Bowl, it is always the same feeling. It's a feeling of emptiness, hopelessness, and utter despair, knowing that the upcoming eight months without football will feel something like being sent to the front line in a war, with two bullets and no gun. These are feelings that can be understood only if you are a full-fledged football fanatic, as I am.

I breathe, eat, and sleep football. When I can no longer perform any of these three things, then, and only then, will I stop loving and consuming myself with football. Then again, if I do stop any one of these three things, it will mean only that I now sit in the best seat in the house, right next to God, Spider Lockhart, Doug Kotar, and of course Frank Sinatra. OK, OK, maybe I won't be sitting next to God himself, but I'm sure I'll be in the same pew as Sinatra.

Photo by Seth Dinnerman

I know I should never assume, but I think by now you should have come to the conclusion that I am, clinically, a football lunatic.

My life revolves around football. Even in the dog days of summer, I am counting the

29

Most Yards Passing, Career: Phil Simms, 33,462 yards in 1979–93.

Most Receptions, Career: Joe Morrison, 395 receptions in 1959–72.

days until camp starts and the new season begins. I record every game during the year. If it's a home game, you can find me analyzing every play for about three or four hours after I get home.

Games that I record when I am on the road with Big Blue Travel still get analyzed, but only after I spend some quality time with my three daughters, the "Pizza Girls." I know that may sound corny to you, but you must understand, Daddy has been away all weekend and my babies have missed me. So now you know the truth, but don't spread it around; my little angels really come first, then football.

You see, there is nothing like having three little girls who worship the ground you walk on. In their sweet, innocent eyes, Daddy can do no wrong. I think that's how most of us Giants fans felt about Lawrence Taylor. It never mattered to us what LT did off the field. We knew, come kickoff, he would go all out and will our team to win. I kept asking myself, "What if this guy ever took the game seriously?"

This is a guy who never lifted weights, came to training camp when he wanted to, and would then go out every Sunday and dominate the poor soul, or souls, who tried to stop him. He had a gift that will live forever in the hearts of every Giants fan lucky enough to have lived through his era and watched in amazement as he played the game of football at a completely different level than the rest. I think the way my angels look at me, like a statue on a pedestal, is in a lot of ways the way we used to view LT. He was bigger than life in the eyes of the innocent. No matter how many chips in the marble, the statue would never crumble.

In the Beginning

I have been a New York Giants fan since September 23, 1961, the day I was born. My folks are fond of saying that I came out of the womb waving a Giants pennant and chanting, "Dee-fense! Dee-fense!" Fortunately, I have been blessed with the best parents in the world. Certainly for their wisdom and neverending compassion, but specifically because they have been Giants season-ticket holders since 1959. Most new-borns get rattles or silver spoons to play with; for me, having been born into a Big Blue Tailgating Family, a spatula and a pair of tongs were my favorite toys, and believe it or not, I've been cooking ever since. Needless to say, I have been the envy of all who know me for quite some time.

So why am I qualified to be an authority on tailgating?

As a kid growing up in Bensonhurst, Brooklyn, your heart had better belong to a New York sports team or you are an outcast of your neighborhood, not to mention the shame of your family. You had one choice, and that one choice was no choice. You rooted in season for the Yankees, the Rangers, and the Knicks, and then there was the fall and the New York Football Giants. The families and kids in my neighborhood who weren't lucky enough to have season tickets went to church on Sundays and made sure the sauce and meatballs were cooking. The sauce and meatballs were for watching the game on TV (or listening on the radio if there wasn't a sellout and the game wasn't televised), and would be timed perfectly with the start of halftime and consumed in fifteen minutes so you wouldn't miss the start of the third quarter. My family, on the

Photo by Linda Kosarin

Giants' All-Time Leading Scorer: Placekicker Pete Gogolak, 646 points in 1966–74.

First Giants Elected to Hall of Fame: Founder Tim Mara and center Mel Hein were elected as charter members of the hall in 1963.

other hand, went to the Giants games and always made sure the car was packed for a Monster Tailgate party. Mom and Dad belong in the Tailgater's Hall of Fame.

Like most Giants fans, I rejoice in the team's winning seasons and suffer terribly through the losing ones. Back in the late sixties and through the seventies, the Giants were a pretty lousy football team. During those difficult years, the best part of the game wasn't really the game at all, but the tailgate party. On the way home from another depressing loss at Yankee Stadium we would begin to plan the next game's tailgate. (I can still hear Dick Lynch on the radio saying, "It's a sad Giants locker room.")

Through the years I have taken my tailgating very seriously. In the lean Giants years, the joy of tailgating sustained my friends and me while we waited and prayed for a winner. In the good years a great tailgate party made the winning that much more enjoyable. So, in the heat of summer, when the sun broils the streets of Bensonhurst, I dream of the parking lots at the Meadowlands. Whether it will be a winning or a losing season no one knows, but what I do know is that there will be tailgating. Old friends and new will gather at their appointed spots, acquaintances will be renewed, and the smell of delicious food will be in the air.

Join me, good friends and fans, in the wonderful world of tailgating. Look for me, Willie the "Pizza Man" Mariano, on the NFL highlight reels, join me and the group from Big Blue Travel on our away-game trips, or stop by the parking lot and watch the master of the Monster Tailgate party at work.

I'll try to provide you with everything you'll need to have a successful tailgate, and it's a great way for me to share with you the truly fantastic times I've experienced throughout my years as a die-hard Big Blue football fan.

May all your tailgate feasts be a "Giant" success! Meet you in the parking lot. Mangia!

The "Pizza Man"

The New York Giants Tailgating Corps

We are the elite, the chosen multitude, 76,000 strong, The New York Giants Tailgating Corps. Prior to the start of the preseason we begin our rituals. We look at them as a type of Parris Island boot camp of the Meadowlands, a reinforcement of our commitment to the rigors of preparing for another tailgating season.

We are the proud, the faithful, the N.Y.G.T.C.

Through the long months of spring and summer we develop our plan of battle. We focus on our strategy for supporting our team as they seek out their NFL enemies and attempt to destroy them. We are the rear-echelon battalions who support our team and help them persevere, no matter what the odds are against us.

We are the proud, the faithful, the N.Y.G.T.C.

It is in our veins and in our souls to always be "True Blue."

We agonize over NFL battles lost and rejoice in games won.

We never retreat from the one-hundred-yard battlefield of the Meadowlands.

You are the battle-hardened soldiers and I applaud you, from my fellow fans who don hard hats like I do, to the guy in the gorilla suit in section 138, and to all the rest of you troops who wear your colors with pride and conviction. We sometimes don't know each other's names, and yet we are joined by football

Photo by Seth Dinnerman

33

Pro Football's First Televised Game: October 22, 1939. The game was broadcast by NBC and was held at Brooklyn's Ebbetts Field. The Brooklyn Dodgers beat the Philadelphia Eagles, 23–14. The game, broadcast to the lucky five-hundred-or-so New York homes that had tel-evisions, went out over NBC's experi-mental station W2XBS. Many others saw the game at the RCA Pavilion at the New York World's Fair.

forces unexplainable by this mere mortal. We are all part of this unparalleled army.

I sense this every time I walk into Giants Stadium. I have come to realize this special bond among Giants fans by my experiences at road games. It is a bond that cannot be matched in any other stadium in the NFL. When other teams' so-called fans go to their seats, that's just what they do—go to their seats. When you are at Giants Stadium, on the other hand, it is like a fraternity party, from the parking lot all the way to your seat. This is evident as we pass one another and acknowledge our passion for our team with eye contact and a heck of a lot of hooting and hollering. Even an outsider can feel that something special and magical is going on.

We stand together as one, never letting our faith waver. We always look to find the good in our team, even when times are bad. (And, as long-time Giants fans, boy, do we know bad.) When the team wins for us, there are no better fans on the planet, but when they lose, we can be brutal. Anyone who ever played, or plays, for the G-men can never hold our pas-sion against us and can only conclude that we are the truest and bluest fans there are.

We will always stand behind our beloved "Big Blue" as long as we see an effort and desire to be the best. In today's foot-ball world, there are not many players left who play just for the love of the game. Our support and our pride runs deep simply because we are the proud, the faithful, the New York Giants Tailgating Corps. Semper Fi. Hoorah!

Tailgating Basics

Photo by Linda Kosarin

Photo by Linda Kosarin

Photo by Linda Kosarin

Let's Get Cookin'!

As a tailgate purist, I prefer a good old-fashioned charcoal briquette grill. For some of you, using traditional charcoal may not be a practical or convenient way to tailgate. Therefore, a gas grill is what you'll need to begin a successful tailgate.

There are many new and exotic tools for barbecuing that are quite expensive. I stick with the original basic tools, long-handled tongs, a spatula, a fork, a sharp knife, and oven mitts. (Football fans may be macho, but we're not stupid.)

You'll need folding tables and chairs that are compact enough to fit in your trunk and still leave plenty of room for food and your cooler full of beverages.

As any good Boy Scout knows, it pays to always be prepared. Always carry a tarp with your tailgate supplies, in case of bad weather. All you need is four poles and four sandbags, and you have yourself a tent to dine in.

Leave an extra roll of aluminum foil in your trunk to wrap leftovers for taking home or into the stadium to munch on during the game.

Always have plenty of antacid tablets in your glove compartment. Believe me when I say that they come in pretty handy for that long trip home, especially after a loss. Just ask an Eagles fan.

And please, whatever you may forget to bring, don't forget the football to toss around while the food cooks!

Photo by Seth Dinnerman

37

More Historical Facts

First Giants Monday Night Game: The Giants played their first-ever Monday night game on November 23, 1970. Norm Snead, who would later become a Giants quarterback, led the Philadelphia Eagles to a 23–20 victory.

Tailgate Checklist

- ✓ GAME TICKETS
- ✓ GRILL
- ✓ CHARCOAL/PROPANE
- ✓ MATCHES/LIGHTER FLUID
- ✓ COOKING UTENSILS
- ✓ OVEN MITT
- ✓ TABLE/CHAIRS
- ✓ TABLE COVER (PAPER/CLOTH)
- ✓ PREPARED FOODS
- ✓ ICE
- ✓ BEVERAGES
- ✓ PLASTIC/PAPER CUPS
- ✓ PLASTIC/PAPER PLATES
- ✓ KNIVES/FORKS/SPOONS
- ✓ NAPKINS
- ✓ PAPER TOWELS
- ✓ PREMOISTENED TOWLETTES
- ✓ ALUMINUM FOIL
- ✓ PLASTIC WRAP
- ✓ CONDIMENTS
- ✓ TRASH BAGS
- ✓ RECYCLE BAG OR CAN
- ✓ PORTABLE RADIO/TV
- ✓ ANTACID TABLETS
- ✓ FIRST AID KIT
- ✓ WATER FOR WASHING UTENSILS
- ✓ TARP/SAND BAGS/POLES
- ✓ DESIGNATED DRIVER

Tailgate Food Safety

Although the tailgating experience is designed to provide enjoyment to the game-day rituals, precautions must be taken by the food providers and cooks to ensure the best presentations of their food. It is important to recognize the dangers in serving certain dishes without proper preparation or storage.

Bacteria are everywhere, especially on foods of animal origin. While often you can't see, smell, or taste them, with the right conditions bacteria such as E. coli and salmonella can grow quickly, spoil food, and make you very sick. You want to avoid dangerous food-borne illnesses such as botulism. Scientists have discovered a particular temperature "danger zone" between 40° F and 140° F. This range covers basically the time and temperature from when food is removed from the refrigerator to before it begins to cook. If food is transported without an ice source, such as a cooler, or left out in the hot sun for any prolonged length of time, it may not remain safe to consume. Food-borne illnesses are frequently misdiagnosed as a form of "summer flu" bug because symptoms are flu-like.

Follow the Pizza Man's basic food preparation tips to ensure a safer tailgating experience!

Photo by Seth Dinnerman

- Try to plan the right amount of food to take to your tailgate party. Too little food and your guests will be hungry. Too much food and you have to concern yourself about the storage or safety of leftovers.

- Wash your hands well and be sure all work surfaces and utensils have been thoroughly cleaned before preparing food. You might want to add an extra jug of water to your tailgating checklist for this purpose.

- If you plan to cook food ahead of time, be sure to allow plenty of time for the food to chill thoroughly in the refrigerator before transporting it. Pack the food from the refrigerator right to the coolers you will be taking to the game. Make sure that there is plenty of ice or ice packs to keep food at 40° F or lower.

- If you must take the tailgater's "low road" and decide to serve take-out foods such as fried chicken or store-bought prepared barbecue beef, you should eat them within two hours of purchase. If you want to pick up this kind of food beforehand, make certain that you allow enough time for it to chill sufficiently in the refrigerator before you pack it in a cooler. Remember to have plenty of ice in the cooler to keep it at 40° F or a slightly lower temperature.

- Don't put your coolers in the trunk. On a summer day it can get hot in a car trunk. Put the coolers in the air-conditioned car backseat.

- At the stadium, try to keep your coolers in the shade and try to avoid repeated openings. Make sure to replace ice as it melts.

Raw meats and poultry need special handling.

- Pack individual servings of poultry or meats in separate plastic bags if possible. This will greatly decrease the chances of contamination. Before you begin to cook, remove only the amount of poultry or meat that will fit on your grill. Do not eat raw or undercooked ground beef since harmful bacteria may be lingering.

- Cook burgers and ribs to 160° F (about medium done) until there is no pink in the center and the juice is clear to ensure that bacteria have been destroyed. Reheat precooked meats until steaming hot.

40

- Cook poultry parts to 180° F and ground poultry to 165° F.

- Don't partially cook extra burgers to use later. Once you start to cook them, finish the job. This will ensure that all the bacteria will be destroyed.

- When you are ready to take cooked food off the grill, be sure to put it on clean plates. Do not put cooked food on a platter that held raw meat or poultry.

  If you plan to marinate your meat, fish, or poultry, be aware that the uncooked meat, fish, or poultry in the marinade is highly perishable.

- Always marinate fish, poultry, or meat in a covered container in the refrigerator.

- Do not marinate for more than twenty-four hours.

- Throw out any leftover marinade.

  Salads, deli meats, and foods need to be kept cold.

- Keep cold foods cold (40° F or below).

- Deli meats have a short shelf life. Roast beef, chicken breasts, and turkey have a shorter refrigerator life than processed meats or cold cuts.

- Salads or other dishes that contain eggs or mayonnaise are especially vulnerable to rapid bacteria growth when left out in the hot sun. Be sure to place in coolers when not being used.

The most important rule for food safety that the Pizza Man can offer his Big Blue tailgating brothers and sisters is: When in doubt . . . throw it out!

First Super Bowl: In 1967. The champions of the upstart American Football League, the Kansas City Chiefs, played the NFL champion Green Bay Packers in the AFL-NFL World Championship game (later named the Super Bowl, after a child's toy, the Super Ball) at the Los Angeles Coliseum. The Packers beat the Chiefs 35–10. Tickets for the game were only $10 each.

The Ten Commandments of Tailgating

I   Thou shalt always remember to buy beer on the Saturday before game day; you may not be able to get it on Sunday.

II   Thou shalt use the Lord's name in vain only if the First Commandment is broken.

III   Thou shalt always get to the parking lot early and still leave plenty of time to go into the stadium to pump up your favorite players. Just verbal abuse, and no profanity, please!

IV   Thou shalt never use flowers and candles as a centerpiece for your table. That's for opera fans. Real football fans use food for a centerpiece. Remember: The more food on the table, the better the feast for the beasts.

V   Thou shalt never bring quiche to a tailgate, because to bend a well-known phrase, "Real fans don't eat quiche."

VI   Thou shalt always tailgate no matter what the weather or your team's record. Sometimes the best part of the game is the tailgate.

VII   Thou shalt never bring trail mix to a tailgate. This health food stuff is not food for football fans: it's for squirrels, rabbits, and chipmunks.

VIII   Thou shalt always be sure to attend church on Saturday night so you can get to the game early enough to fulfill the Third Commandment.

IX   Thou shalt always pack enough food for the surprise guests (usually relatives) who show up with nothing more than a bottle of soda and a bag of chips.

X   Thou shalt never have the same tailgate cookout twice in one season; being different is good. Besides, if you have the same tailgate more than once, there's less of a chance for *The NY Giants Fan Guide to Tailgating, Book 2.*

Chef, Chief—It's All How You Look at It

Here are some rules all chefs live by, and all tailgaters must adhere to!

- The chef is right.

- The chef is always right, no matter what!

- The chef never eats; he only nourishes himself.

- The chef only sips; he never drinks.

- The chef is never late; he is only delayed.

- The chef is never criticized.

- Unless the chef changes his mind, his decisions are final.

- If you have any problems with any of the above rules, find another chef!

Photo by Linda Kosarin

43

Terms of (Bar-B-Q) Endearment

Pitmaster: The artist who turns meats into delicious barbecue by working his or her magic over the hot coals.

Closed Pit Barbecue: A pit in which the meat is cooked in an enclosed space, with the heat and smoke combining with the meat from either a direct or indirect fire.

Open Pit Barbecue: A pit in which the meat is placed directly over hardwood coals at a distance of one to four feet.

Wood Burner: One who makes barbecue by burning hardwoods down to coals for use as the source of heat and smoke.

Basting Sauce: Liquid added to the meat during barbecuing to add moisture and flavor. Usually applied with a small mop-type brush. A.k.a.: mopping sauce, sopping sauce.

Finishing Sauce: A sauce applied to barbecue just before it is eaten. A.k.a.: dip, table sauce.

Marinades: A liquid flavoring composed of acids (like citrus juices or vinegar), oil, and spices, used to marinate food before cooking. Not as common as dry rubs in barbecuing.

Photo by Seth Dinnerman

Rubs: Dry, powdery seasonings that are rubbed into the meat before cooking to add zest, seal in flavors, and produce a tasty crust.

Slather: A pasty wet version of a dry rub used to add moisture and to apply a milder taste than dry rubs.

Miss White: The light, moist inside of pork barbecue.

Mister Brown: The dark, smoky outside of pork barbecue.

44

The Tailgating Trinity

Hamburgers, Hot Dogs, & Heros

Photo by Mike Malarkey

Photo by Seth Dinnerman

How the Hamburger Got Its Name

Call it whatever you like—Big Mac, Whopper, slider—it really doesn't matter. Charbroil it, steam it, fry it, add heaping helpings of onion, lettuce, tomato, ketchup, or mustard, slip a couple of pickle slices onto a fresh roll, and you have joined the royal court of King Hamburger. More than thirty-eight billion hamburgers were served in 1998. Statistically, that comes to thirty pounds of hamburger consumed by every American, an average of three burgers a week. Sometimes I feel as if I must cook half those burgers in a given year at my Monster Tailgate parties. So how did this king of all foods fast and easy come into being? No one is entirely sure who ate the first hamburger, but in the dreary off-season days, the Pizza Man frequently contemplates this question. Maybe some caveman long, long ago found an animal that had been hit by lightning and wound up well-done. The first taste might have been different from what he was used to, but I'll bet the smile on his face was the same as ours today when he realized what he had.

Let's jump forward to the recent past, say maybe the last thousand years or so. The Tartars and Genghis Khan's warriors rode the land that is now Russia and Mongolia. These nomads just loved the taste of raw steak. Uncooked meat, however, is usually pretty tough. To tenderize it, they used to take their raw steaks, season them, and place them under the saddles on the backs of their horses. After a hard day of riding across the steppes, fighting and pillaging, they would remove the now tender meat and enjoy their

Photo by Seth Dinnerman

47

dinner. Today, at a fancy restaurant, you could spend $25 or more for a similar delicacy called Steak Tartare. Go figure!

So now we jump to the early 1900s, when immigrants from Germany carried recipes for Hamburg-style chopped steak from the old country. By 1910, the "hamburger" was widely eaten and had come to be known by that name. In 1921, Billy Ingram and his partner, Walter Anderson, steam-fried small burgers (they weighed less than an ounce and cost a nickel) with a formula that became the foundation of the country's first burger chain, White Castle.

America's love affair with the hamburger really took off when a milk shake-machine salesman named Ray Kroc teamed up with two brothers named McDonald in 1948. The rest is history. Fifty years later, McDonald's is right up there with corporations like Microsoft and IBM.

Through the years, the hamburger has proven itself to be the fast food of choice in America.

Photo by Linda Kosarin

Hamburgers

Blitz Burgers

3 pounds ground beef sirloin
1 box (2.4 ounces, 2 envelopes) dry onion soup mix
1/4 cup water
Salt and pepper to taste
Vegetable oil
6 potato hamburger rolls
Ketchup, mustard, pickles, sliced tomato to taste

At home: In large plastic bag, mix ground beef, both envelopes soup mix, and water until well combined. Seal tightly and refrigerate overnight.

At the game: Preheat grill to medium heat. Shape meat mixture into 6 football-shaped patties. Place on grill. Brush generously with oil. Grill burgers 4 to 8 minutes. Turn and brush with oil. Cook 4 to 8 minutes more or until of desired doneness. Toast buns, if desired. Serve on toasted bun topped with ketchup, mustard, pickles, and tomatoes to taste. Makes 6 servings.

Tailgate tip: If you forget to pack a basting brush, have no fear. Just hold your thumb over the opening of the bottle and sprinkle.

NOTE: For additional servings add 8 ounces ground meat per serving. Season with additional onion soup mix if desired.

To my crew, this is just a snack,
So the more you grill, the more they'll be back.
You must blitz them with side dishes that are easy to prepare,
The more you have, the more you can share.

Understanding Free Agency

UFA: Unrestricted free agent. Player who has finished four or more tenured seasons of service and whose contract has ended, thereby making him free to sign with any team through July 15. On July 16, his exclusive rights return to his original team if that team makes him a June 1 tender offer. His old team has until the tenth week of the season to sign him. If he does not sign by then, he must stay out the season. If no tender is offered, he can be signed by any team at any time throughout the season.

How the Hot Dog Got Its Name

Sometime around 1852, the local butchers' guild in Frankfurt, Germany, created a spicy smoked sausage packed in a skin casing and named it a frankfurter. The curved shape of the sausage supposedly looked like the dachshund dog of one of the butchers, and the frankfurter was sometimes called a "dachshund sausage."

The frankfurter's introduction to America is credited to Charles Feltman, a baker in Coney Island, Brooklyn, around 1910. Feltman's bakery couldn't survive the competition from the hotels and restaurants that served meals there, so he decided to sell one kind of hot food from a pushcart: the frankfurter. His idea was such a hit that he was able to open a German beer garden in 1913. One of the people he hired was another immigrant, Nathan Handwerker. In 1916, Handwerker opened his own stand, using his wife's recipe and offering his franks at a nickel each, half the price of those sold by his former boss. Since that day, Nathan's Famous has become a Coney Island landmark and a national chain.

Hot Dogs

Halfback Hot Dogs

2 packages (16 ounces each) frankfurters (all-beef, pork and beef, chicken, etc.)
16 frankfurter rolls, cut in half lengthwise
1 package (16 ounces) sauerkraut, lightly drained
Mustard, ketchup, relish, shredded cheese to taste

At home: Place sauerkraut in flame-proof casserole or saucepan. Cover tightly.

At the game: Preheat grill to medium-low heat. Place sauerkraut on grill. Place dogs on grill and stand by with your long-handled fork. Cook 5 to 10 minutes, turning to brown evenly. The key here is to keep those doggies rollin', rollin', rollin,' so they don't char. Toast roll, if desired. Serve on roll with hot sauerkraut, mustard, etc. Makes 10 to 12 servings.

Tailgate tip: For chili dogs, top with heated homemade or canned chili. Be sure to have lots of napkins.

Along with Blitz Burgers, Halfback Hot Dogs are a snack,
So stuff them with chili or Monterey Jack.
It's quick and it's easy to have a good meal,
Clean up is easy, it's no big deal!

RFA: Restricted free agent. Player who has finished three tenured seasons of service and whose contract has ended. Player has received a qualifying offer from his old team and is free to negotiate with any team until April 13, at which time his rights return to his original team. If a player accepts an offer from a new team, the old team will have the right to match the offer and retain the player. If the old team chooses not to match the offer, they may receive draft-choice compensation, depending on the level of the qualifying offer made to the player.

How the Sandwich Got Its Name

In the early eighteenth century, a gentleman gambler by the name of John Montagu enjoyed many a night at the gaming tables of various European gambling establishments. He was a serious gambler who didn't like to leave the table when he was playing. To ease his frequent hunger pangs, Montagu, a member of British nobility known by his title, the Earl of Sandwich, used to order slices of meat between two slices of bread. The simple but satisfying meal he frequently requested has been passed down through the years to become the reigning king of fast foods: the sandwich.

The "Italian hero" sandwich, a.k.a. submarine, hoagie, poor boy, grinder, or any other name applied by those unsophisticated souls outside the New York metropolitan area, originated in Naples, Italy, as a small meat and cheese sandwich on a relatively small roll.

The most accepted version of how the Italian hero came to be called a hoagie has its roots in Philadelphia. Hog Island, an area of Philadelphia that was home to a shipyard at the turn of the century, employed a lot of Italian immigrants. These immigrant workers, nicknamed hoagies, brought giant sandwiches made from large loaves of Italian bread, cold cuts, spices, olive oil, lettuce, tomatoes, onions, and peppers.

As time passed, the name became attached to the sandwich but somehow wound up with a different spelling. (Why, you ask? Hey, we're talking people from Philly, ya know!)

While we're talking about Philadelphia, a convenience store chain called WaWa launched a petition campaign in 1992 to name the hoagie the official sandwich of Philadelphia. Thirty-five thousand people signed the petition. This chain also hosts an annual Hoagie Day celebration. They created a giant 500-foot-long hoagie at the first event and subsequent years have brought larger hoagies. Now, the Pizza Man hosts some

Monster Tailgate parties at which he serves some major sandwiches, but this is a little beyond my capabilities, only because I can't fit it in my truck. Here is the list of ingredients for "The World's Largest Italian Hero."

740 pounds Italian ham

812 pounds prosciutto

704 pounds provolone cheese

672 pounds Genoa salami

672 pounds shredded lettuce

975 pounds tomatoes

503 pounds sliced onion

13 pounds oregano

26 gallons olive oil

19,000 hoagie rolls

A huge dash of salt and pepper

The sandwich weighs 3.8 tons and will feed 19,000 people.

"The secret to a hero is always the bread,
Like a good night's sleep on a warm soft bed.
The inside should be fluffy, the outside golden brown,
Remember once you build one, don't look at it, just chow down."

EFA: Exclusive-right free agent. Player with two or less years of experience who has no outside bargaining clout. His rights belong to his 1997 team, provided they make him a minimum qualifying offer, which varies based on tenure.

Heros

Stacey Robinson's Polish Sausage Heros

Stacey Robinson — (WR) North Dakota State. A number two draft pick in 1985. With Giants from 1985 to 1988. In my opinion, one of, if not the best clutch receivers the Giants ever had. A major contributor to both Super Bowl victories. Born February 19, 1962.

1/4 cup vegetable oil (or olive oil)
12 medium onions, cut into 1/2-inch wedges
6 red bell peppers, seeded and cut into strips
6 green bell peppers, seeded and cut into strips
5 pounds hot and /or sweet Polish sausage
2 loaves (12 ounces each) Italian bread, cut in half lengthwise

At home: In large skillet heat oil over medium heat. Add onions and peppers; cook, stirring occasionally, until lightly browned. Cool and place in heat-proof casserole or saucepan. Cover and refrigerate.

At the game: Preheat grill to medium-low heat. Place sausage on grill. Cook 20 to 25 minutes or until cooked through. Meanwhile, place casserole or saucepan with onion-pepper mixture on grill in a steel pot or aluminum foil. Cook, stirring occasionally, until heated through. Toast bread cut side down, if desired. Cut sausage into serving pieces; serve on bread topped with heated onion-pepper mixture. Makes 8 to 10 servings.

Tailgate tip: To tell if the sausage is done, cut a slice into the sausage and check that it's no longer pink.

The aroma of sausage to a tailgater is heaven,
Like scoring a touchdown, "putting up seven."
Great for the days when winter has arrived,
I guarantee while eating it, you'll be thankful you're alive.

Heros

Potato and Egg Hero

4 tablespoons olive or other vegetable oil
6-8 medium red bliss potatoes, peeled and cut into thin wedges
12 to 16 eggs
3/4 cup milk or water
Salt and pepper to taste
6-8 hero rolls, cut in half lengthwise
Paprika for garnish

At home: In large skillet over medium heat cook potatoes in hot oil until lightly browned, turning once. Drain off excess oil. In bowl mix eggs, milk, and salt and pepper until well combined; pour into skillet with potatoes. Cook until egg is set and potatoes are tender. Sprinkle with paprika. Divide evenly between rolls. Wrap tightly in foil.

At the game: Unwrap and enjoy. Heat over hot grill, if desired.

Tailgate tip: To have sandwiches hot and ready to eat, make just before leaving, wrap tightly, and place in insulated bag.

Heros

Mighty Meatball Hero

1 pound ground beef
1 cup dried bread crumbs
2 eggs
1/4 cup white wine
2 cloves garlic, minced
1 tsp. dried parsley
1 tsp. grated Parmesan cheese
1 large (12 ounces) loaf Italian bread or 4-5 small hero rolls

At home: In large bowl mix ingredients until well combined. Shape mixture into football-type shapes or traditional meatballs. In large skillet add several tablespoons vegetable oil and cook in batches until evenly browned. Add to Mariano's Marinara Sauce with meatballs (recipe on page 128). Place sauce and meatballs in tightly covered container; place in insulated bag.

At the game: Place heated meatballs and sauce on loaf or hero rolls, serve immediately. Makes 4 to 6 servings.

Tailgate tip: If desired, make up heros at home and wrap tightly in foil. To serve hot, heat over hot grill.

Heros

Pizza Man's Deli Supreme Hero

1 pound smoked mozzarella
1 jar (16 ounces) sweet or hot peppers
2 loaves (12 ounces each) Italian bread, cut in half lengthwise
1 bottle (8 ounces) prepared oil and red wine vinegar salad dressing
1 pound thinly sliced Genoa or other salami
1 pound thinly sliced olive loaf

At home: Cut mozzarella into thin slices; wrap tightly. Seed and cut peppers into 2-inch strips; return to jar to store and carry.

At the game: Place bottom halves of bread on work surface. Sprinkle bread evenly with salad dressing. Layer salami, mozzarella, olive loaf, and peppers. Cover with top of bread. Cut into serving pieces. Makes 6 to 8 servings.

Tailgate tip: Feel free to substitute with your favorite deli meats or poultry and salad dressing. Anything goes.

NOTE: The above amounts are a starting point, add more or less as desired.

Hometown Heros: New York Giants Retired Jerseys

Throughout their illustrious history the New York Giants have retired several jersey numbers. Players whose numbers have been retired have had significant impact on the team's history and have been acknowledged as fan favorites.

Jersey Number	Name	Position	Years with Giants
No. 1	Ray Flaherty	End-Asst. Coach *	1928–35
No. 7	Mel Hein	Center-LB *	1931–45
No. 11	Phil Simms	Quarterback	1979–93
No. 14	Y. A. Tittle	Quarterback *	1961–64
No. 32	Al Blozis	Tackle	1942–44
No. 40	Joe Morrison	End-Halfback	1959–72
No. 42	Charlie Conerly	Quarterback	1948–61
No. 50	Ken Strong	Fullback-Kicker*	1933–35/ 1939–47
No. 56	Lawrence Taylor	Linebacker	1981–94

* Denotes Hall of Fame members

Giants in the Hall of Fame:

Morris (Red) Badgro: *No. 17*
End—6-0, 190 pounds (Southern California)
1927 New York Yankees (Football)
1930–1935 New York Giants
1936 Brooklyn Dodgers (Football)
Enshrined 1981.
Played rookie year with Red Grange, 1927 Yankees. Excellent blocker, superior defender, big play receiver. Oldest player ever elected to Hall of Fame. Born December 1, 1902.

Roosevelt (Rosey) Brown: *No. 79*
Offensive Tackle—6-3, 255 pounds (Morgan State)
1953–1965 New York Giants
Enshrined 1975.
Black All-American Morgan State, 1951–1952. Excellent downfield blocker, classic pass protector, big, fast, and mobile. All-NFL eight straight years, 1956–1963. Played in nine Pro Bowl games. NFL's Lineman of the Year, 1956. Born October 20, 1932.

Frank Gifford: *No. 16*
Halfback, Flanker—6-1, 195 pounds (Southern California)
1952–1960, 1962–1964 New York Giants
Enshrined 1977.
All-American at USC. Number 1 draft pick, 1952. All-NFL four years. NFL Player of Year. Seven Pro Bowls. Totaled 9,753 combined yards. Born August 16, 1930.

Mel Hein: *No. 7*
Center—6-2, 225 pounds (Washington State)
1931–1945 New York Giants
Charter Enshrinee, 1963.
1930 All-American. Sixty-minute regular for fifteen years. Never missed a game. All-NFL eight straight years, 1933–1940.

Photos courtesy of the New York Giants

59

NFL's Most Valuable Player, 1938. Flawless ball-snapper, extremely powerful blocker, superior pass defender. Born August 22, 1909. Died January 31, 1992.

Sam Huff: *No. 70*
Linebacker—6-1, 230 pounds (West Virginia)
1956–1963 New York Giants
1964–1967, 1969 Washington Redskins
Enshrined 1978.
All-American guard at West Virginia. Number 3 draft pick, 1956. Great speed. Inspirational leader. Noted for his hard-hitting duels with the likes of Jim Brown and Paul Hornung. Redefined the middle linebacker position. Thirty career interceptions. Played in six NFL title games, five Pro Bowls. All-NFL four years. Top NFL lineman, 1959. Born October 4, 1934.

Alphonse (Tuffy) Leemans: *No. 4*
Halfback-Fullback—6-0, 200 pounds (Oregon, George Washington)
1936–1943 New York Giants
Enshrined 1978.
Second-round pick in first NFL draft. 1936 College All-Star game MVP. Dedicated team leader. Player-coach, 1934 season. 1936 rookie year led all NFL rushers. 5,908 yards combined career yardage total. Threw sixteen touchdown passes and had a fourteen-yard career punt return average. Born November 12, 1912. Died January 19, 1979.

Tim Mara:
Founder-Administrator
1925–1959 New York Giants
Charter Enshrinee 1963.
Bought Giants Franchise in 1925 and provided the NFL with a showcase team in the country's largest city. Built Giants into a perennial powerhouse with three NFL and eight divisional titles. Born July 29, 1887. Died February 17, 1959.

Photos courtesy of the New York Giants

Wellington Mara:
Owner-Administrator
1937–present New York Giants (Fordham)
Enshrined 1977.
Spent entire adult life with Giants. Became President and Co-Chief Executive Officer in 1991. Utilizing his extensive organizational skills, Mara's involvement with player personnel, trading, and drafting led the Giants to sixteen divisional titles, six NFL titles, and two Super Bowls. NFC President, 1984–present. Born August 14, 1916.

(Stout) Steve Owen:
Coach-Tackle—6-2, 235 pounds (Phillips University)
1924–1925 Kansas City Cowboys
1925 Cleveland Bulldogs
1926–1953 New York Giants
Enshrined 1966.
Great defensive star of the 1920s. Coached Giants for twenty-three years, from 1931 to 1953. Career coaching record: 153-108-17, eight divisional, and two NFL championship teams. Credited with developing the A-formation offense, umbrella defense, and the two-platoon system. Born April 21, 1898. Died May 17, 1964.

Andy Robustelli: *No. 81*
Defensive End—6-0, 230 pounds (Arnold College)
1951–1955 Los Angeles Rams
1956–1964 New York Giants
Enshrined 1971.
Superb pass rusher. Smart, quick, and strong. Recovered twenty-two career fumbles. All-NFL seven years. Named NFL's top player by Maxwell Club, 1962. Missed only one game in fourteen years. Born December 6, 1925.

Photos courtesy of the New York Giants

Ken Strong: *No. 50*
Halfback—5-11, 210 pounds (New York University)
1929–1932 Staten Island Stapletons
1933–1935, 1939, 1944–1947 New York Giants
1936–1937 New York Yanks (AFL)
Enshrined 1967.
New York University All-American, 1928. Excelled in every aspect of game. All-NFL, 1934. Led NFL in field goals, 1944. Scored sixty-four points to lead NFL, 1933. Scored seventeen points in famous "sneakers" title game, 1934. Born April 21, 1906. Died October 5, 1979.

Fran Tarkenton: *No. 10*
Quarterback—6-0, 185 pounds (Georgia)
1961–1966, 1972–1978 Minnesota Vikings
1967–1971 New York Giants
Enshrined 1986.
Exciting, elusive scrambler. Threw four touchdown passes in first professional game, 1961. Attempted 6,467 passes, completed 3,686 for 47,003 yards and 342 touchdowns. Also rushed for 3,674 yards and 32 touchdowns. Led Vikings to three Super Bowls. Four-time All-NFL. Selected to Pro Bowl nine times. Born February 3, 1940.

Yalberton Abraham (Y. A.) Tittle: *No. 14*
Quarterback—6-0, 200 pounds (Louisiana State)
1948–1949 Baltimore Colts (AAFC)
1950 Baltimore Colts (NFL)
1951–1960 San Francisco 49ers
1961–1964 New York Giants
Enshrined 1971.
AAFC Rookie of the Year, 1948. Led Giants to division titles in 1961, 1962, 1963. Threw thirty-three touchdown passes in 1962, thirty-six in 1963. NFL Most Valuable Player in 1961, 1963. All-NFL, 1957, 1962, 1963. Six Pro Bowls. Born October 24, 1926.

Emlen Tunnell: *No. 45*
Defensive Back—6-1, 200 pounds (Toledo, Iowa)
1948–1958 New York Giants
1959–1961 Green Bay Packers
Enshrined 1967.
Tunnell was known as the Giants' "offense on defense." Gained more yards in 1952 on interceptions and kick returns than the NFL rushing leader. Held career records in interceptions (79 for 1,282 yards), punt returns (258 for 2,209 yards). All-NFL four years. Nine Pro Bowls. Named NFL's All-Time Safety, 1969. Born March 29, 1925. Died July 22, 1975.

Arnie Weinmeister: *No. 73*
Defensive Tackle—6-4, 235 pounds (Washington)
1948 New York Yankees (AAFC)
1949 Brooklyn-New York Yankees (AAFC)
1950–1953 New York Giants
Enshrined 1984.
One of the best defensive tackles of his time. Big, extremely fast, great mobility, great ability to diagnose plays. All-AAFC, 1949. All-NFL, 1950-1953. Four Pro Bowls. Born March 23, 1923.

Lawrence Taylor: *No. 56*
Linebacker—6-1, 220 pounds (North Carolina)
1981–1994 New York Giants
Enshrined 1999.
NFC Rookie of the Year. Ten-time consecutive All-Pro Selection. Arguably the best defensive player to ever play the game. Single-handedly helped reshape the concept of linebacker play. Born February 4, 1959.

Photos courtesy of the New York Giants

Several other players and coaches who have played or coached for the Giants are in the Hall of Fame through affiliations with other teams.

Pete Henry—
Tackle, 1927
Elected in 1963

Cal Hubbard—
Tackle, 1927–28,
1936 Elected in 1963

Larry Csonka—
Running Back,
1976–78
Elected in 1987

Jim Thorpe—
Halfback, 1925
Elected in 1963

Joe Guyon—
Halfback, 1927
Elected in 1966

Don Maynard—
End, 1958
Elected in 1987

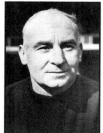

Hugh McElhenny—
Halfback, 1963
Elected in 1970

Vince Lombardi—
Asst. Coach, 1954–55
Elected in 1971

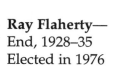

Ray Flaherty—
End, 1928–35
Elected in 1976

Tom Landry—
Defensive Back,
1950–55
Elected in 1990

Photos courtesy of the New York Giants

A Spider to the Rescue

There were many magical moments in 1986, the best season the New York Football Giants ever achieved, from the amazing fourth and seventeen in Minnesota to the fluke touchdown in the Super Bowl by fan favorite Phil McConkey. (You remember, the one that bounced off Mark Bavaro's chest into Phil's arms to ice the victory.)

If you were to ask Giants fans what they remember best about this unforgettable season, you will get thousands of different answers. To me, the one image that personifies this dream season was the play that most fans can remember vividly.

What you're about to read can make or break my reputation as a sane individual. It was a play in the 1986 Divisional Playoff game against the 49ers that sort of went unnoticed, unless you were there and were a true-blue dedicated Giants fan, as we all were that day. This one play told every Giants fan in attendance that fate was on our side. It was a play that made more than seventy-five thousand people believers in divine intervention.

Allow me to take you back thirteen years. This was a time, for those of you who can remember, when New York City was alive and vibrant with successful sports teams. Of course, there were none that came close to catching the hearts of millions like our New York Football Giants. Going into the 1986 season, most Giants fans believed that this was the year, if everyone stayed healthy, that would be a very special season indeed. This of course was never more evident than in that Divisional Playoff game versus the 49ers.

The play, which occurred in the first few minutes of the game on the 49ers' second possession, started at the 49ers' eighteen-yard line. Giants Stadium was electric. I had never before felt the feeling of sheer euphoria and confidence going into any game involving my beloved Giants as I did that day. I mean, these were the Lawrence Taylor-led Giants, on a mission that no mortal soul or souls would be able to derail.

Understanding Free Agency

FP: Franchise player. A team can assign one franchise player, who must be offered a minimum of the average of the top five salaries at the player's position, or 120 percent of the player's previous year's salary, whichever is greater. If the player is offered a minimum of the average of the top five salaries of last season at his position, he can negotiate with other teams. His old team can match a new team's offer or receive two first-round draft choices if they decide not to match. An "exclusive" franchise player is not free to sign with another team.

I can still feel the stadium rocking; the noise from the frenzied crowd was so loud that both teams had trouble hearing their signals. Then came The Play. Joe Montana took two steps from center and hit a slanting Jerry Rice across the middle.

Rice was behind our secondary, cradling the football and sprinting right at me, toward the end zone I'm sitting in, when suddenly at about the twenty-five-yard line, the football seemed to mysteriously pop right out of the hands of a shocked Jerry Rice. He tried to scoop up the ball as he continued toward the end zone. After bobbling it a few times he was hit by three Giants, and Gary Reasons recovered the ball in the end zone. Touchback, Giants ball.

This is what was seen by the naked eye, but more than half the stadium knew better. You see, there was this eerie feeling that came over the crowd that not ten seconds before had stood holding its breath in stunned silence. As we watched in horror, Rice was galloping toward what would have been a 7–0 lead, when that itsy-bitsy spider came down from its heavenly web and snatched the ball away.

I am told today by everyone who was at the game (even by those who watched on television) that they were sure they had witnessed some sort of unknown phenomenon on that bitterly cold December day. Most agree that it was the great Spider Lockhart who came down from the heavens to pluck the ball from Rice's unsuspecting arms. If you can recall, this was the year that our team wore patches on their jerseys bearing the number forty-three and a spider. So why, I ask, could this not be fact? There are countless others who agree that I'm not out of my mind to feel this way. Who am I to deny

Photo by Seth Dinnerman

66

the fact that something so out of the ordinary could happen in front of some seventy-five thousand rabid fans?

You might be saying to yourself, this Pizza Dude is a few slices short of a whole pie, but do you have a better explanation as to why one of the greatest wide receivers of our time suddenly dropped the football with not a single Giant within twenty yards of him? I believe to this day, and will continue to until someone proves me wrong, that Spider saw the play and said, "No way are we gonna get cheated out of this Super Bowl journey the way we did in the Windy City last year." So he reached down from his tailgate in the sky and stopped Rice's premature celebration right in his tracks. To this, I simply say, "Thanks, Spider."

The only other explanation I can come up with is that Jerry Rice is not a teamster union type of guy and Jimmy Hoffa, rumored to be buried in the Meadowlands, saw to it that Rice would not upset this Super Season, therefore guaranteeing that our lunch-pail, blue-collared Giants would fulfill their dreams and reach the ultimate goal of being Super Bowl champions.

TP: Transition player. A player who must receive a minimum of the average of the top ten salaries of last season at his position, or 120 percent of his previous year's salary, whichever is greater. Present teams maintain a first-refusal right to match any bids from new teams within seven days of the signing of an offer sheet after the player's contract expires. If the team matches, they retain the player. If they do not match, they receive no compensation.

67

Smelling Dad's Steaks

Photo by Seth Dinnerman

Photo by Seth Dinnerman

Photo by Seth Dinnerman

Smelling Dad's Steaks

For as long as I can remember, I have been attending tailgate parties at Giants football games. It seems like only yesterday that Mom, Dad, and all of their football friends were partying in the parking lots of Yankee Stadium. I can still smell Dad's specialty—marinated steak and onions—sizzling on his homemade grill. Mom and Dad were masters of the fine art of tailgating. It explains why I take so much pride in my tailgate parties. I take my tailgating seriously, and when I invite my crew and friends I don't expect much—just bring your appetite, appreciate the effort that goes into one of my tailgates, and show up. When a guy in my crew or an invited guest calls me on Sunday morning to say he isn't coming to my tailgate because it's too cold or snowy, tough luck, he's never invited again. You may think this is too harsh a punishment, but you have to realize how much preparation goes into one of my Monster Tailgate parties. I even go to the trouble of finding little football plates and napkins so one would feel the ambiance of a true football party. I know I may be a bit excessive, but, hey, who's the one writing the book here, me or you? Well, I hope you agree with me and will use this book as a guide to help make your future tailgates a huge success.

Now, back to dear old Dad's succulent steaks cooking to perfection on his homemade grill. To me there was no better sight. The grill was about three feet wide and at least six feet long, with a cooking space of 2,592 square inches. Now that's a lot of grilling space. Dad used to have two to three dozen steaks sizzling at any given time on those sacred Sundays. Yankee Stadium is a truly magical place, and I often found

Photo by Seth Dinnerman

myself thinking of the legendary Yankees and Giants players who played on that sacred turf in their glory days. How could you not, when so many sports legends have gone through those steel gates leading to the Players Only entrance? I started going to Giants Football games when I was nine or ten years old, and the Giants weren't such a great team back in the late sixties and seventies. As a matter of fact they were pretty darn awful. Our quarterbacks at the time couldn't hit water if they fell out of a boat.

We were so ineffective that nobody wanted to let us play on their field. Yankee Stadium told us to go away, so we had to share Shea Stadium with the Jets. I guess New York City figured we would never become a contender and opted to allow the state of New Jersey to woo the Giants to the Meadowlands. In between, we were forced to go wherever our team did, from Yankee Stadium in the Bronx to Shea Stadium in Queens and all the way to the Yale Bowl in Connecticut. It never mattered how far we had to travel, though. If there was a Giants game being played in Moosebreath, North Dakota, we still would have packed our cars and driven for as long as it took to get there to tailgate.

Photo by Seth Dinnerman

Beef

Charles Way's Fullback Beef Ribs

Charles Way — (FB) Virginia. Drafted in the sixth round (206th pick overall). With Giants from 1995 to present. A bruising fullback who punishes defenders. Charles has stepped into a leadership role on the team, and has brought new energy to the offense. Born December 27, 1972.

Photo by Jim Turner

4 cups water
3/4 cup granulated sugar
1/2 cup firmly-packed dark brown sugar
1 1/3 cups tomato paste
2/3 cup honey
2/3 cup prepared mustard
1/3 cup red vinegar
6-8 pounds beef spareribs

At home: To make barbecue sauce: In large saucepot over high heat bring water to boil. Add sugars; stir until sugars are dissolved. Add tomato paste, honey, mustard and vinegar. Reduce heat to low; cook, stirring occasionally, 2 hours. Remove from heat and cool slightly. Meanwhile, in Dutch oven place pork spareribs and enough water to cover. Bring to a boil over high heat. Reduce heat to low; cover and simmer 45 to 60 minutes or until just tender. Drain. Place ribs in large shallow storage container or plastic bag; add barbecue sauce. Cover or secure tightly and refrigerate overnight.

At the game: Preheat grill to medium to low heat. Lightly drain ribs, reserving remaining barbecue sauce. Place on grill. Cook 15 to 20 minutes or until heated through; turn and brush with any remaining sauce about every 15 minutes. Cut into serving pieces. Makes 6 to 8 servings.

Tailgate tip: To eliminate the loss of marinades, cover grill with aluminum foil and punch holes for ventilation.

> *Charles is a guy who comes to play,*
> *He leaves defenders in dismay.*
> *These ribs are for bruisers like Mr. Way,*
> *When you eat them they'll make your day.*

Beef

Backfield Bacon-wrapped Filet Mignon

6 center-cut filet mignon steaks, cut 1 1/2-inch thick (about 6 to 8 ounces each)
6 slices Canadian bacon
Small metal skewers or toothpicks
1 can or bottle (12 ounces) strong-flavored beer
1/2 cup balsamic vinegar
1 clove garlic, crushed
Salt to taste

At home: Wrap edges of each individual steak with slice of bacon; secure with skewer or toothpick. Set aside. In shallow storage container that will hold steaks in single layer, combine beer, vinegar, garlic, and salt. Add meat. Cover and marinate overnight in refrigerator.

At the game: Preheat grill to medium-hot heat. Lightly drain steak, reserving marinade. Place steaks on grill. Brush with marinade. Cook 10 minutes; turn and brush with any remaining marinade. Cook 6 to 8 minutes more for rare, 10 to 12 minutes for medium.

Tailgate tip: If desired, use small wood skewers to secure bacon. Use tongs to handle and turn meat.

NOTE: To insure the bacon is cooked, hold steaks on edge and turn carefully during last 5 minutes of grilling.

Here's a dish that's fit for a king,
Through dead of winter or days like spring.
A meal that is sure for all mouths to catch,
A recipe, bar none, that's real hard to match.

Beef

Kickoff Kabobs (beef)

5 pounds top or bottom round beef, cut into 1-inch cubes
1 can (12 ounces) beer (imported is nice)
1 cup red wine
3 large yellow bell peppers, seeded and cut into 2-inch squares
3 large red bell peppers, seeded and cut into 2-inch squares
1 large Bermuda or other sweet onion, cut into 2-inch squares
24 large mushrooms, stems removed
12 metal or wood skewers

At home: In large shallow storage container or plastic bag combine beef cubes, beer, and wine. Cover or secure tightly and refrigerate overnight. Prepare vegetables and place in storage container or plastic bags. Cover or secure tightly.

At the game: Preheat grill to medium-hot heat. On each skewer place mushroom cap, beef, yellow pepper, beef, red pepper, beef, onion, beef. Repeat until skewer is full, ending with mushroom cap. Grill 15 minutes or until of desired doneness, brushing with remaining marinade and turning to brown all sides. Makes 8 to 10 servings.

Tailgate tip: To prevent wood skewers from burning, soak in water for 10 to 15 minutes before using.

NOTE: To do in one step, thread meat and vegetables on skewers, then marinate in wine-beer mixture overnight. Grill as above.

There's nothing like a shish kabob,
Although preparing them is quite a job.
Be creative and free and add your own flair,
And I'll guarantee by game time, the skewers will be bare.

Beef

Super Bowl Sirloin

1 sirloin steak, cut 1- to 1 1/2-inch thick (about 3 pounds)
1 bottle (8 ounces) prepared Italian salad dressing

At home: In large shallow storage container or plastic bag place steak and salad dressing. Cover or seal tightly and refrigerate overnight.

At the game: Preheat grill to medium-hot heat. Lightly drain steak, reserving marinade. Place steaks on grill. Brush with marinade. Cook 10 minutes; turn and brush with any remaining marinade. Cook 6 to 8 minutes more for rare, 10 to 12 minutes for medium. Makes 6 to 8 servings.

Tailgate tip: Slice this up thin and serve with natural juices on thick sliced bread or hero rolls. Great with "Super Bowl Salad" (page 152) on side.

This one's for all those friends of mine,
Who always tailgate rain or shine.
A marinated steak on the path to the Bowl,
To celebrate not watching your cholesterol.

Beef

Swing Pass Steak

6 to 8 sirloin steaks, cut 1 1/4 -inch thick (about 6 to 8 ounces each)
1 cup soy sauce
2 cloves garlic, crushed
1/2 cup strained baby apricots

At home: In large shallow storage container or plastic bag place steaks, soy sauce, and garlic. Cover or seal tightly and refrigerate overnight.

At the game: Preheat grill to medium heat. Place steaks on grill. Brush with strained apricots. Cook 10 minutes; turn and brush with remaining strained apricots. Cook 6 to 8 minutes more for rare, 10 to 12 minutes for medium. Makes 6 to 8 servings.

Tailgate tip: Keep a spray bottle of water close by to douse any flames that may flare up due to dripping fat.

NOTE: Carefully watch the steaks; if the coals are too hot the sugar in the apricots may char and burn.

When I first tried this dish I was afraid of the fruit,
But I cannot lie, I must tell the truth.
It's named "swing pass steak" 'cause it went for a score,
Inside ten minutes the steak was no more.

Beef

Illegal Chuck Steak

1 large onion, finely chopped (about 1 cup)
1 cup ketchup
1/3 cup firmly-packed brown sugar
1/3 cup red wine vinegar
1 tablespoon Worcestershire sauce
1/4 to 1/2 teaspoon dried crushed red pepper
1 well-trimmed beef chuck T-bone steak, cut 3/4- to 1-inch thick (about 2 pounds)

At home: To make barbecue sauce: in bowl or measuring cup combine onion, ketchup, brown sugar, vinegar, Worcestershire, and crushed red pepper to taste. In large shallow storage container or plastic bag place 1 cup barbecue sauce and steak. Cover or seal tightly and refrigerate overnight. Cover and refrigerate remaining barbecue sauce.

At the game: Preheat grill to medium heat. Lightly drain steak. Place steak on grill. Cook 15 to 18 minutes for medium rare or until of desired doneness. Meanwhile, place reserved barbecue sauce in heat-proof casserole or saucepan on grill. Cook, stirring occasionally, until bubbling. Remove steak from grill; slice. Serve sliced steak with heated barbecue sauce. Makes 4 to 6 servings.

Tailgate tip: For more servings add an extra steak and make extra barbecue sauce. Barbecue sauce can be made ahead of time and stored in the refrigerator up to 3 to 4 days.

Beef

Touchdown Teriyaki

3 pounds beef flank steak, cut into bite-sized serving pieces or strips
2 cups prepared teriyaki sauce
6 medium tomatoes, cut into fourths
4 large red or other sweet onions, cut into 3/4-inch slices
2 large green bell peppers, seeded and cut into 1-inch slices
2 large red bell peppers, seeded and cut into 1-inch slices
8 metal or wood skewers

At home: In large shallow storage container or plastic bag combine flank steak and teriyaki sauce. Cover or secure tightly and refrigerate overnight. Prepare vegetables and place in storage container or plastic bags. Cover or secure tightly.

At the game: Preheat grill to medium-hot heat. Lightly drain steak, reserving marinade. On each skewer alternate tomatoes, beef, onion, green pepper, beef, red pepper, and beef. Repeat until skewer is full. Grill 15 minutes or until of desired doneness, brush with remaining marinade, and turn to brown all sides. Makes 8 servings.

Tailgate tip: For easier handling and less trouble threading on the skewers, cut the onions in half lengthwise, then into thick wedges.

NOTE: If tomatoes are very ripe, add them to the end of the skewer during last 5 minutes of cooking time.

You're here for football not for hockey,
You're bound to love my Touchdown Teriyaki,
Too many beers and you might get rocky,
So try this dish with some warm sake.

Beef

Flanker Right Marinated Flank Steak

1 flank steak, about 3 pounds
3 small Bermuda onions, finely chopped
1 cup vegetable oil
1/2 cup soy sauce
2 cloves garlic, minced
4 to 5 tablespoons honey
3 to 4 tablespoons vinegar
Salt and pepper to taste

At home: In large shallow storage container or plastic bag combine onions, oil, soy sauce, garlic, honey, vinegar, salt, and pepper. Add steak. Cover or seal tightly and refrigerate overnight.

At the game: Preheat grill to medium-hot heat. Lightly drain steak, reserving remaining sauce. Place steak on grill. Cook 5 to 7 minutes; turn and brush with remaining sauce. Cook 5 to 7 minutes more or until of desired doneness. Cut on diagonal into thin slices. Makes 8 to 10 servings.

Tailgate tip: Any remaining marinade should be heated to boiling on the grill before serving over cooked steak.

This one is for the meat lovers like me,
Who love a good steak as much as a victory.
When cooked with care it's like no other,
It will cut with a fork and melt like butter.

Beef

Grandma Jennie's Giant Meatloaf

2 pounds chopped sirloin
4 eggs, lightly beaten
4 medium carrots, peeled and shredded
1 cup cooked long-grain white rice
1 cup dry seasoned bread crumbs
4 cloves garlic, minced
2 teaspoons dried parsley
4 strips bacon, if desired
1 can (16 ounces) tomato sauce
2 medium onions, thinly sliced
Sugar to taste
Oregano to taste
1 can (16 ounces) peas, drained

At home: Preheat oven to 350° F. In large bowl, mix beef, eggs, carrots, rice, bread crumbs, garlic, and parsley until well combined. In large baking pan shape meat into football-shaped loaf (longer than thicker). Top with bacon, if desired. In small bowl stir tomato sauce, onions, sugar, and oregano. Pour into baking pan around loaf. Bake 20 minutes. Add peas. Bake 10 to 20 minutes more or until cooked through. Let stand 10 minutes. Place in container or wrap tightly in foil.

At the game: Slice. Reheat on grill if desired. Makes 8 to 10 servings.

Tailgate tip: Great to make ahead of time and freeze. Defrost a day before serving. Serve cold, thinly sliced on crusty bread or hero rolls with lettuce, tomato, and pickle.

Pork

Rodney Hampton's Running Back Ribs

Rodney Hampton—(RB) Georgia. Drafted in the first round (24th pick overall). With Giants from 1990 to 1997. Holds Giants' record for the most consecutive 1,000-yard rushing seasons. Also holds the all-time Giants' rushing record with 1,842 attempts for 6,897 yards, 49 touchdowns, and a career 3.8 yards-per-carry average. Rodney never stopped trying for those extra yards and carried the team for most of his career. Born April 3, 1969.

Photo by Jim Turner

4 cups water
3/4 cup granulated sugar
1/2 cup firmly-packed dark brown sugar
1 1/3 cups tomato paste
2/3 cup soy sauce
2/3 cup prepared mustard
1/3 cup white vinegar
6 to 8 pounds pork spareribs or pork loin back ribs

At home: *To make barbecue sauce: In large saucepot over high heat bring water to boil. Add sugars; stir until sugars are dissolved. Add tomato paste, soy sauce, mustard, and vinegar. Reduce heat to low; cook, stirring occasionally, 2 hours. Remove from heat and cool slightly. Meanwhile, in Dutch oven place pork spareribs and enough water to cover. Bring to a boil over high heat. Reduce heat to low; cover and simmer 45 to 60 minutes or until just tender. Drain. Place ribs in large shallow storage container or plastic bag; add barbecue sauce. Cover or secure tightly and refrigerate overnight.*

At the game: *Preheat grill to low to medium heat. Lightly drain ribs, reserving remaining barbecue sauce. Place on grill. Cook 35 to 45 minutes or until heated through; turn and brush with any remaining sauce about every 15 minutes. Cut into serving pieces. Makes 6 to 8 servings.*

Tailgate tip: *To eliminate the loss of marinade, cover grill with aluminum foil and punch holes for ventilation.*

This dish is not for the nicely dressed,
So wear a bib to catch the mess.
But, please be civilized, 'cause I will not condone
Hitting opposing fans with the leftover bones.

Pork

Point-After Pork Chops in Salsa

1 jar (16 ounces) prepared tomato salsa
5 medium carrots, peeled and shredded
8 green onions, thinly sliced or chopped
6 to 8 center-cut loin pork chops, about 1-inch thick

At home: In large shallow storage container or plastic bag combine salsa, carrots, and green onions. Add pork chops. Cover or seal tightly and refrigerate overnight.

At the game: Preheat grill to medium-hot heat. Lightly drain pork chops, reserving remaining sauce. Place pork on grill. Cook 15 to 25 minutes or until no longer pink, turn, and brush with remaining sauce. Meanwhile, place heat-proof casserole or saucepan with remaining salsa mixture on grill. Cook, stirring occasionally, until heated through. Serve chops with heated salsa mixture. Makes 6 to 8 servings.

Tailgate tip: If desired, thinner 3/4-inch pork chops can be used. Cook as directed above for only 10 to 12 minutes.

This one is called the other white meat,
If not overcooked it's tender and sweet.
Most of your guests will line up for more,
This point-after dish is really a score.

Pork

Lawrence Taylor's Rum Raisin Pork Chops

Lawrence Taylor — (LB) North Carolina University. Number two draft pick in 1981. With Giants from 1981 to 1994. Only pro player to appear in ten consecutive Pro Bowls. Voted the NFL's MVP in 1986, the first defensive player to win since 1971. Led Giants to two Super Bowl victories. Finished career with 142 sacks, among the all-time leaders. On October 10, 1994, his No. 56 jersey was retired by the Giants. On January 30, 1999, he was elected to the Pro Football Hall of Fame on a first ballot in his first year of eligibility. He was certainly the greatest player I have ever seen. Born February 4, 1959.

Photo by Jim Turner

3/4 cup orange juice
3/4 cup rum
2 tablespoons brown sugar
1/4 teaspoon each ground nutmeg and cloves, if desired
Salt and pepper to taste
6 to 8 center-cut loin pork chops, about 1/2-inch thick
1 cup dark seedless raisins

At home: *In large shallow storage container or plastic bag combine orange juice, rum, brown sugar, nutmeg, cloves, salt, and pepper. Add pork chops and raisins. Cover or seal tightly and refrigerate at least 6 hours or overnight.*

At the game: *Preheat grill to medium-hot heat. Lightly drain pork chops, reserving remaining marinade. Place pork on grill. Cook 3 to 5 minutes. Turn and brush with some remaining marinade; cook 3 to 5 minutes or until no longer pink. Meanwhile, place heat-proof casserole or saucepan with remaining marinade and raisins on grill. Cook, stirring occasionally, until heated through. Serve chops with heated raisin mixture. Makes 6 to 8 servings.*

Tailgate tip: *If desired, add a bit of cornstarch mixed with water to remaining marinade with raisins to thicken. If a large quantity of sauce is desired, double the amount of marinade and raisins.*

'Editor's Note: Following is the speech that the Pizza Man delivered at a banquet hosted by Big Blue Travel (the official road trip company of the Giants) to mark the retirement of the greatest linebacker ever to play the game of football, Lawrence Taylor.

The Pizza Man had been trying for months to convince Big Blue Travel to include a fan's perspective. He had faxed Michael Martocci numerous times about the subject, and finally Michael relented and invited the Pizza Man to speak at LT's retirement. On the dais were notables like Mike Francesa of WFAN, Leroy Neiman, Lawrence himself, and of course the Pizza Man. After all the assembled talent offered their tributes, it was the Pizza Man's turn. Willie the Pizza Man, dressed in his finest No. 56 jersey and hand-painted hard hat, and clutching the statue of Saint Lorenzo Taylor, delivered the following and absolutely brought the house down. Everyone in the room appreciated the fan's fan, and the tribute he offered to the greatest of all Giants, Lawrence Taylor.

First of all, I'd like to thank Mike Martocci and everyone here—I am honored to represent all Giants fans across America to pay tribute to this man. While most of you talk about Lawrence's greatness and athletic achievements, I've got a story nobody knows.

I gotta tell you something, Lawrence, when you came to the Giants you got me in big trouble with my grandma, but I stood up for you, I redeemed you. You see, on her dresser she had a typical Italian grandmother's shrine of saints. St. Rocco, St. Anthony, St. Peter, St. Paul—you name the saint, it was on her dresser.

What do I do? One night I come home from a game and it's pretty late. It was a typical

Taylor night, typical Monster Tailgate party. I win this little statue of Lawrence on a bet with my friends. I put it on grandma's dresser with the rest of the saints. Marone, Fuggedaboutit, you don't know what I went through! It was like an inquisition. I had to have a sit down with all of Brooklyn, my Uncle Rocco from the Bronx, my Uncle Vito from Staten Island . . . you owe me, Lawrence, you don't know how much. I convinced grandma and the rest of them that there was a Saint Lorenzo Taylor from Virginia who played for the football Giants.

As a proud Italian-American from Bensonhurst, which often gets a bad rap in the media, and you know all about bad raps, I know I speak for all Giants fans when I say we truly love you and wish you were still here. If only there was a way to turn back the clock, but that hasn't been discovered yet. Lawrence, you have an open invitation to my neighborhood because you are a symbol of achievement for all humanity. If Grandma Angie were alive today, she would cook you a feast fit for the "King of Saints." And one other thing, Lawrence, this hard hat, which you personally signed at a card show in Bensonhurst in the 80s, I take off to you anytime, anyplace, anywhere.

Photo by Seth Dinnerman

Pork

Power Sweep Pork Tenderloin

1 clove garlic
1 boneless pork loin roast (about 3 1/2 to 4 pounds)
1 package (6 to 8 ounces) sauerkraut, drained
1 large onion, finely chopped
1 large red apple, cored and coarsely chopped
1 can or bottle (12 ounces) beer
Salt and pepper to taste

At home: Cut garlic clove in half lengthwise; rub over pork roast. Set aside. In large shallow storage container or plastic bag combine sauerkraut, onion, apple, beer, and salt and pepper to taste. Add pork roast. Cover or seal tightly and refrigerate overnight.

At the game: Preheat grill to medium-hot heat. Lightly drain pork roast, reserving remaining sauerkraut mixture. Place pork on grill. Cook 20 to 25 minutes or until no longer pink, turning 3 to 4 times. Meanwhile, place heat-proof casserole or saucepan with sauerkraut mixture on grill. Cook, stirring occasionally, until bubbling. Remove roast from grill; slice. Serve sliced pork with heated sauerkraut mixture. Makes 6 to 8 servings.

Tailgate tip: Using charcoal briquettes that are treated to automatically start prevents having to carry flammable charcoal lighter fluid in the car.

NOTE: If desired, whiskey can be substituted for beer. Roast may cook faster.

Veal

Victory Veal Marsala

1 1/2 pounds veal cutlets (milk-fed are nice), cut into serving pieces
1 1/4 cups all-purpose flour
1/4 to 1/2 cup Marsala wine
Lemon slices, if desired
Salt and pepper to taste

At home: Pound veal until 1/4 inch thick. Coat veal with mixture of flour, salt, and pepper. Place in large shallow plastic container. Pour in Marsala wine. Cover or seal tightly and refrigerate overnight.

At the game: Preheat grill to medium-hot heat. Lightly drain veal cutlets. Place cutlets on grill. Cook 4 to 5 minutes per side or until tender. Serve with lemon slices. Makes 6 servings.

Tailgate tip: If you prefer, chicken or turkey cutlets can be substituted for veal. Prepare as directed above.

Toochie

Whatever comes out of this fantasy trip that I have been on for the last few years, one thing is evident: I have been living every football fan's dream. In these last three years, starting in 1995, I have been on ten Giants road trips and have attended countless other functions. From celebrity dinners with the 1986 Giants and current players to charity functions with the legendary Yogi Berra and Joe DiMaggio—all this and so much more, courtesy of the greatest road trip company this side of the moon, Big Blue Travel.

You see, as I already mentioned in my dedication, 1995 was the year I met Michael Martocci. I hope that after reading my dedication you can understand how big a place he has in my heart. This is a man who not only gives more than he has, but he does so without wanting anything in return. If he were down to his last two bucks and he knew you needed one, he would give you both. I'm sure he knows that I too would give him my last dollar.

The friendship we have developed has nothing to do with money and everything to do with the mutual respect we have for each other. This respect comes from knowing just how difficult it is to make it from the streets of Brooklyn, and when you do, not forgetting where you came from.

Now you tell me if this friendship came about out of sheer luck, or fate? After running into one closed door after another while trying to get more deeply involved in Giants fan events, I would not allow my determination to diminish. You see, I firmly believe that the more doors that are

Photo by Seth Dinnerman

89

closed in your face, the more doors will open for you. That is, of course, provided that you don't stop knocking on the doors. So here is a little tip from a guy who doesn't know much. If you are tenacious enough and persistent in your approach, and if you can get over the doors being slammed in your face, you too can achieve whatever it is you set out to do (pretty profound from a paisan from Bensonhurst, eh?).

The point I am trying to make is that you never know what you might find behind a closed door if you don't knock on it, open it, or kick it down.

To my good fortune, behind one of my doors stood a guy I fondly call the King of New York. I know there must be many who lay claim to this title, but believe me there is only one. I call Michael this not because of his riches, but for the loyalty and generosity he shows to those he cares for.

Without Michael, I would be just another schlep from Bensonhurst who dreams but never achieves. So if I sound like I love this guy, I do! You got a problem with that?

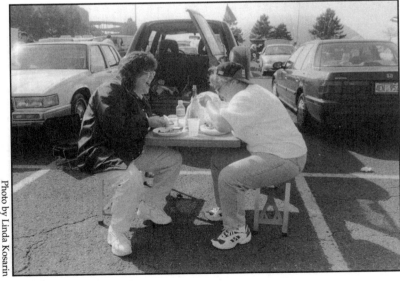

Photo by Linda Kosarin

90

Personal Fowl

Photo by Mike Malarkey

Photo by Linda Kosarin

The Origin of the Rubber Chicken

Back in the late seventies and early eighties, when I first started going to Giants games on a regular basis, the Giants were not a very good football team. In fact, we were pretty awful. These were the times when the tailgate parties were, more often than not, far more exciting than the games. The team was so feeble that we, the faithful, would do anything to try to amuse ourselves. It was a major chore just to get through four quarters of miserable football without going insane. We were starving for some action, no matter what form it came in.

One Sunday, very late in the season on a bitterly cold December day, our beloved Giants were in the middle of taking their weekly bashing. We were sitting there freezing our tails off, desperate for anything to cheer for just so we could warm up, when out of nowhere strolled this tiny blue bird. Half of our section (105), along with sections 104 and 106, started to cheer this little critter on. As he got closer to the goal line, the cheers grew louder. I can remember seeing all of the media people on our side of the field, along with the players on the bench, turning to see what was going on. When this little fella crossed the goal line, the roar you heard from the crowd was louder than any that had ever been heard before in the then-new home of the New York Football Giants.

Photo by Seth Dinnerman

This bird started to play the crowd as if he knew the cheers were for him. He continued going back to the five-yard line, turning and looking at the crowd, and then racing across the goal line. The cheers soon turned to laughter, and by then everyone in the stadium was watching this cute little blue bird score touchdown after touchdown. I couldn't even tell you how badly the Giants lost that day, because all we could remember was the bird.

At the next home game, a lot of the fans were looking for the bird. To our disappointment, he never showed up. So for the following home game, my brother bought a rubber chicken, painstakingly painted it in Giants colors, attached a little plastic Giants helmet (the ones you used to get in bubble gum machines) to its head with a rubber band, and started a trend that would continue right up until 1986. This rubber chicken became our little good luck charm and was in Pasadena on January 25, 1987, the day we won our first Super Bowl. Say what you may about superstitions and rituals, but hey, it's obvious that it worked. So now you know it was the chicken and not the tuna that helped us with the big one.

Photo by Seth Dinnerman

Chicken

Game-breaking Grilled Chicken

8 skinless, boneless chicken breast halves (about 2 pounds)
Salt and pepper to taste
2/3 cup honey
3 tablespoons spicy brown mustard
8 hamburger buns or hard rolls, if desired
Sliced tomato, if desired

At home: Season chicken with salt and pepper. In large shallow storage container or plastic bag combine honey and mustard. Add seasoned chicken. Cover or seal tightly and refrigerate overnight.

At the game: Preheat grill to medium heat. Remove chicken, reserving remaining honey-mustard mixture. Place chicken on grill. Cook 12 to 15 minutes or until cooked through; turn and brush with remaining honey-mustard mixture. Serve on bun with sliced tomato, if desired. Makes 8 servings.

Tailgate tip: If desired, grilled chicken can be thinly sliced on the diagonal and served over a bed of mixed greens for a tempting main-dish salad.

NOTE: If you prefer, turkey cutlets or 1/2-inch slices of boneless pork can be substituted for chicken. Prepare as directed above.

A real easy dish for those on the go,
You need not be a chef for this one, you know.
The honey and mustard make quite a nice taste,
I'm sure with this one, there will be no waste.

Chicken

Kickoff Kabobs (chicken)

2 to 3 pounds boneless, skinless chicken, cut into 1-inch cubes
1/4 cup lemon juice
3 large green bell peppers, seeded and cut into 2-inch squares
3 large red bell peppers, seeded and cut into 2-inch squares
2 cans (20 ounces each) pineapple chunks in syrup or juice, drained
24 large mushrooms, stems removed
12 metal or wood skewers

At home: On each skewer place mushroom cap, chicken, green pepper, chicken, red pepper, chicken, pineapple, chicken. Repeat until skewer is full, ending with mushroom cap. In large shallow storage container place prepared kabobs. Sprinkle with lemon juice. Cover or secure tightly and refrigerate overnight.

At the game: Preheat grill to medium-hot heat. Place kabobs on grill. Cook 8 to 10 minutes or until cooked through, turning occasionally. Makes 8 to 10 servings.

Tailgate tip: If desired, substitute pineapple juice, teriyaki sauce, soy sauce, or prepared salad dressing for lemon juice. Prepare as directed above.

Here is one that takes great patience,
But when done right, is loved by all nations.
Most might think it's just for summer,
But to deny this year-round to friends would be a bummer.

Chicken

Punt Return Parmigiana Chicken

8 to 10 boneless, skinless chicken breast halves, flattened
Salt and pepper to taste
2 large eggs
1/2 cup milk or water
1 to 1 1/2 cups seasoned bread crumbs
1/2 to 1 cup vegetable oil
3 cups prepared marinara or Mariano's Marinara Sauce (page 128)
1 package (16 ounces) mozzarella cheese, shredded or thinly sliced

At home: Lightly grease large flame-proof casserole or baking pan; set aside. Season chicken breasts with salt and pepper; set aside. In shallow dish or bowl beat eggs and milk until well combined. On waxed paper or dish place bread crumbs. Meanwhile, in large skillet over medium heat, heat several tablespoons oil until hot. Dip chicken pieces in egg mixture then bread crumbs to evenly coat. Place in skillet in single layer; cook until lightly brown and almost cooked through, turning once. Remove and place in prepared casserole. Repeat with remaining oil and coated chicken. Top with marinara sauce then sprinkle with mozzarella cheese. Cover tightly and refrigerate overnight.

At the game: Preheat grill to medium-hot heat. Place casserole of chicken on grill. Cover and cook 15 to 20 minutes or until heated through and cheese melts. Makes 8 to 10 servings.

Tailgate tip: Prepare in disposable aluminum baking pan for ease of cooking and clean up.

NOTE: Chicken can be covered with foil on an open grill or cooked uncovered with the grill top down.

> This is one that's not so easy,
> All the frying can make you queasy.
> An Italian tradition that is quite a meal,
> All who eat it will know it's the real deal.

Chicken

Post Pattern Pineapple Chicken

8 skinless, boneless chicken breast halves (about 2 pounds)
Salt and pepper to taste
1 cup orange juice
2 to 3 tablespoons olive oil
2 large cloves garlic, crushed
1 fresh pineapple, peeled and cut into slices, or 2 cans (20 ounces each) pineapple slices, drained

At home: Season chicken with salt and pepper. In large shallow storage container or plastic bag combine orange juice, oil, and garlic. Add seasoned chicken. Cover or seal tightly and refrigerate overnight.

At the game: Preheat grill to medium heat. Remove chicken, reserving remaining orange mixture. Place chicken on grill. Cook 12 to 15 minutes or until chicken is cooked through; turn and brush with remaining orange mixture. Place pineapple on grill during last 2 to 3 minutes; cook until lightly browned, turning once. Serve chicken with pineapple slices. Makes 8 servings.

Chicken

Stuff-the-Run Stuffed Chicken

8 boneless chicken breast halves with skin
Salt and pepper to taste
2 tablespoons olive oil
1 clove garlic, crushed
2 pounds fresh spinach, trimmed, washed, and drained, or 2 packages (10 ounces each) frozen spinach, thawed
2 to 4 tablespoons white zinfandel or other white wine
1 package (8 ounces) mozzarella cheese, cut into 8 stick-like pieces
Toothpicks, small skewers, or cooking string

At home: Pound each chicken breast until 1/8-inch thick. Season with salt and pepper; set aside. In large skillet over medium-high heat cook garlic 1 minute in hot oil. Add spinach and wine. Cook, covered, 3 to 5 minutes or until spinach is limp and cooked through. Cool slightly. In center of each chicken breast place 1/8 spinach mixture and piece of cheese. Fold in side edges and roll up; secure with toothpick or tie with string. Place in shallow storage container and cover or wrap tightly in foil. Refrigerate.

At the game: Preheat grill to medium-hot heat. Place chicken rolls on grill. Cook 15 to 20 minutes or until cooked through and cheese melts; turn occasionally to evenly brown. Makes 8 servings.

Tailgate tip: Serve these chicken rolls with a cold rice or vegetable salad to complete the meal.

A dish that is always fun to prepare,
When done right, has its own fanfare.
A tricky one that takes some time,
If you have trouble rolling, just drink the wine!

Chicken

Tiki Barber (Q) Mustard Chicken

Tiki Barber—(RB) Virginia. Drafted in second round in 1997 (36th pick overall). 1997 to present. Began his rookie season as a starting running back after beating out Tyrone Wheatley in the preseason. Has identical twin brother, Rhonde. They played football together their whole lives, right through college at Virginia, but were separated when they became pros (Rhonde was drafted by the Tampa Bay Buccaneers). Born April 17, 1975.

Photo by Jim Turner

4 to 6 pounds broiler-fryer chicken, cut into serving pieces
Salt and pepper to taste
1/2 cup Dijon mustard
3 tablespoons cider or other vinegar
2 tablespoons molasses or honey
4 teaspoons Worcestershire sauce
1 teaspoon fresh thyme or 1/8 teaspoon dried thyme leaves

At home: *Season chicken with salt and pepper. In large shallow storage container or plastic bag combine mustard, vinegar, molasses, Worcestershire, and thyme. Add seasoned chicken. Cover or seal tightly and refrigerate overnight.*

At the game: *Preheat grill to medium heat. Remove chicken, reserving remaining mustard mixture. Place chicken on grill. Cook 20 to 30 minutes or until chicken is cooked through; turn and brush with remaining mustard mixture. Makes 8 servings.*

Tailgate tip: *Use your favorite chicken piece (thighs, legs, breasts, etc.) for this delicious recipe.*

Turkey

Michael Martocci's Big Blue Turkey Breast

Michael Martocci is the president of Big Blue Travel and one of the nicest people you will ever meet. His heart is always in the right place and the Giants road trips he offers are absolutely first class. When we are on the road and I am hosting Monster Tailgate Parties, Michael insists that I cook his favorite turkey recipe. Here it is.

1 5-pound turkey breast, sliced into 8-ounce pieces
2 cups Balsamic vinegar
1/2 cup olive oil (extra Virgin Italian)
2 tablespoons fresh parsley, chopped finely
1/2 tablespoon basil
3 cloves garlic, chopped
Salt and pepper to taste

At home: Place all ingredients into a large bowl with sealable cover and marinate overnight in refrigerator.

At the game: Place marinated turkey breast on hot grill, cook for five minutes on each side depending on thickness. Turn only once or twice and be careful—turkey cooks fast on a grill. Serve on Italian bread or rolls for a hero, or just in a dish like Michael likes it.

If it's health you crave, this one is it,
A quick, tasty dish that's always a hit.
With an Italian flair as you can see,
What else would you expect from a Martocci?

Duck, It's a Snowball

There are quite a few characters who attend professional football games. Some of them tend to forget what a privilege it is to have New York Football Giants season tickets. I never give up my ticket to a game, but I firmly believe that if you do, you should be very selective as to whom you give your tickets. A prime example of fans not doing this was the last game of the year in the 1995 season. Now, I understand it was two days before Christmas and our record was 5 and 10, but it is no excuse for the way a minority of fans acted the way they did. If you haven't guessed yet, I'm talking about the dreaded snowball game against the San Diego Chargers. To me it was the ultimate embarrassment; I can only imagine how it was for our great organization. I'm telling you something, folks, I was really fortunate to have my hard hat that cold December day. I don't go to Giants games to have popcorn and peanuts and watch the half-time show. I'm there to watch football, and

Photo by Seth Dinnerman

I tend to get really focused and into the game, like most of the faithful Giants fans. Only on this day, a few young men decided to start throwing snowballs. It really got out of hand, as was evident in all those terrible highlights shown across the country. Now, you have to try to picture this. There I was, sitting with a few of my fellow hard-hat buddies in the front row. Something told me to stand up and voice my opinion to these rowdies. How very wrong I was. After telling them in a not-so-nice way to stop throwing snowballs, they bombarded us with snowball after snowball. We ran for cover up all those steps as if we were in a war and had to make it back to the safety of camp. There are a few dents and chips in my hard hat as a result. It should never have happened and can and should be avoided in the future. Please, for the sake of our classy organization, be selective of whom you give your tickets to. If you don't, and it snows, hard hats are mandatory.

From the Sea

Photo by Seth Dinnerman

Photo by Seth Dinnerman

Photo by Seth Dinnerman

Seafood

Sean Landeta's Shellfish and Angel Hair Pasta

Sean Landeta — (P) Towson State University. With Giants from 1985 to 1993. His amazing ability to kick booming punts with long hang times was an integral part of the Giants' successful Super Bowl seasons. Sean has been a longtime favorite of Giants fans, and I have never seen him refuse a request for an autograph. Born January 6, 1962.

4 tablespoons olive or other vegetable oil
2 cloves garlic, minced
8 to 12 medium plum tomatoes, coarsely chopped
1/4 cup packed parsley, chopped
Salt and pepper to taste
1 pound cooked lobster tail meat, cut into cubes
1 pound colossal shrimp, peeled, deveined, and cooked
1 pound bay scallops
1/2 pound lump crabmeat, picked over
2 packages (16 ounces each) angel hair pasta

Photo by Jim Turner

At home: In large saucepan over medium-high heat cook garlic 1 minute in 3 tablespoons hot oil. Add tomatoes, parsley, salt, and pepper. Bring to a boil. Reduce heat to low; simmer 15 minutes. Add lobster, shrimp, scallops, and crabmeat. Cover and cook 7 to 10 minutes or until scallops are cooked and seafood heated through. Place in storage container and cover tightly. Meanwhile, cook angel hair pasta according to package directions. Drain well. Toss with remaining tablespoon oil; place in storage container or plastic bag. Cover or seal tightly.

At the game: In large bowl or pot place hot angel hair pasta. Top with hot sauce and toss to coat. Serve immediately. Makes 8 to 10 servings.

Tailgate tip: Though less fancy, sturdier pasta like thick spaghetti, linguine, or ziti will travel better.

Seafood

Phil McConkey's Grilled Spicy Shrimp

Phil McConkey — (WR) Navy. With Giants from 1984 to 1988. A fearless, intelligent player with great, soft hands. Phil had a knack for being in the right place at the right time. He probably is best remembered for his clutch catch of a touchdown pass that bounced off Mark Bavaro in the end zone, which propelled the Giants to their Super Bowl win. Born February 24, 1957.

Photo by Jim Turner

1 cup safflower or other vegetable oil
1/2 cup lemon juice
1/4 cup honey
1 clove garlic, crushed
1/2 to 1 teaspoon liquid hot pepper sauce
1/2 teaspoon paprika
Salt and pepper to taste
3 pounds jumbo shrimp, peeled and deveined

At home: In large shallow storage container or plastic bag combine oil, lemon juice, honey, garlic, hot pepper sauce, paprika, salt, and pepper. Add shrimp. Cover or seal tightly and refrigerate overnight.

At the game: Preheat grill to medium heat. Cover grill with aluminum foil and punch holes for ventilation. Remove shrimp, reserving remaining marinade. Place shrimp on grill. Cook 4 to 5 minutes or until pink, turn once, and brush with remaining marinade. Makes 8 servings.

Tailgate tip: If desired, thread shrimp on skewers and place on grill. It makes it easy to turn and serve.

Seafood

Coach Fassel's Sideline Shrimp

Head Coach Jim Fassel—Fifteenth head coach in team history. Hired on January 15, 1997. Led the Giants in his first year to a 10–5–1 record, a playoff berth, and the NFC East Championship. Also named NFL Coach of the Year. His stabilizing influence and dedicated work ethic are sure to keep the Giants focused in their hunt for the next Championship season. Coach Fassel is truly a gentleman, and never hesitates to involve himself in charitable causes.

Photo by Linda Kosarin

1/2 cup lemon juice
1/3 cup orange juice
1/3 cup ketchup
1/4 cup honey
1/4 cup safflower or vegetable oil
1 clove garlic, crushed
1 tablespoon soy sauce
1/4 teaspoon paprika
Salt and pepper to taste
3 pounds jumbo shrimp, peeled and deveined

At home: To make barbecue sauce: in blender container or medium bowl blend all ingredients except shrimp until smooth. In large shallow storage container or plastic bag combine barbecue sauce and shrimp. Cover or seal tightly and refrigerate overnight.

At the game: Preheat grill to medium heat. Cover grill with aluminum foil and punch holes for ventilation. Remove shrimp, reserving remaining barbecue sauce. Place shrimp on grill. Cook 4 to 5 minutes or until pink, turn once, and brush with remaining barbecue sauce. Makes 8 servings.

Tailgate tip: For saucier shrimp, heat remaining barbecue sauce and generously brush over shrimp just before serving, or serve heated sauce on the side for dunking.

If it's shrimp you like to eat,
Here's a dish that's quite a treat.
The catch of the day will make your feast,
A gourmet meal, to say the least.

Seafood

Hail Mary Mako

3/4 cup soy sauce
1/2 cup red wine
1 clove garlic, crushed
1/2 teaspoon ground ginger
6 to 8 Mako shark steaks, about 3/4-inch thick

At home: In large shallow storage container or plastic bag combine soy sauce, wine, garlic, and ginger. Add shark steaks. Cover or seal tightly and refrigerate overnight.

At the game: Preheat grill to medium-hot heat. Remove shark steaks, reserving remaining soy-wine mixture. Place shark steaks on grill. Cook 8 to 10 minutes or until fish flakes easily when tested with a fork; turn once and brush with remaining soy-wine mixture. Makes 6 to 8 servings.

Tailgate tip: Be sure to bring a large flat spatula for turning fish and turn carefully to prevent fish from falling apart.

> Here's a dish that's hit or miss,
> For a real fish eater it's always bliss.
> A play that's called when desperate for a win,
> Like its name it's sink or swim.

Seafood

Sehorn Swordfish

Jason Sehorn—(CB) USC. Drafted in second round in 1994. With Giants from 1994 to present. Jason is fast becoming one of the elite defensive players in the NFL. His athletic ability and pure instinct are unparalleled. After missing the entire 1998 season with a devastating knee injury, I am sure Jason will be back in 1999, stronger and better than ever. Born April 15, 1971.

Photo by Jim Turner

2 large tomatoes, diced
1 jar (8 ounces) marinated artichoke hearts
2 small ribs celery, chopped
1 large onion, chopped
8 swordfish steaks (about 6 to 8 ounces each), cut 1-inch thick
Salt and pepper to taste

At home: In large shallow storage container or plastic bag combine tomatoes, artichoke hearts, oil, celery, and onion. Cover or seal tightly. Season swordfish with salt and pepper to taste. Wrap tightly and refrigerate all night.

At the game: Preheat grill to medium-hot heat. Place swordfish on grill. Cook 8 to 10 minutes or until fish flakes easily when tested with a fork; turn once. Meanwhile, place tomato mixture in heat-proof casserole or saucepan on grill. Cook, stirring occasionally, until bubbling. Serve swordfish topped with heated tomato mixture. Makes 6 to 8 servings.

Tailgate tip: If desired, sauce can be cooked ahead of time and seved cold over grilled fish.

A Mile High but Never Green

This story may enhance or destroy my reputation as a True Blue Giants fan. It is something I am not very proud of, so please have a little mercy on me. Most people would kill for a job like mine, so I hope you will understand my dilemma.

I do not need to remind you that our beloved Giants missed the playoffs in 1998. Although missing the playoffs was bad enough, we had to endure one miserable half of a season, in which we lost to the likes of the Raiders and the Redskins. We also had to watch as we became a competitive team late in the season, beating playoff teams like the upstart Cardinals and the defending Super Bowl Champion Broncos.

But it was too little too late, and it was off to the golf course and summer vacation much too early. We did finish the season on a high note though, winning three straight and five out of the last six. A small consolation for a team who won the NFC East just one year before. However, being the ultimate optimist, the future sure looks bright.

Now, my dilemma. As you know, I have the greatest job in the world. It may not pay all that much, but hey, what's money when you do something you really love?

Photo by Seth Dinnerman

Working at Big Blue Travel has allowed me to travel with our beloved Giants and see all the games on the road. The problem I have is that Big Blue Travel wears many hats. We run not only road-trip packages for the Giants, Rangers, Knicks, and Yankees, but also for two teams I call the enemy.

It's difficult enough for me that Big Blue also runs the road-trip company for the 49ers, 49er Fan Tours, but we also handle (hold your breath, folks) the road-trip company for the other tenants of Giants Stadium, the New York Jets, called Jet Getaways. Don't get me wrong, I am far from complaining. I did get to go to Colorado for the AFC Championship game on January 17, 1999, between the Broncos and the Jets. The game in itself was an epic battle and a fight to the finish, but there was no Blue to be found except, of course, in the sky.

The trip involved leading 250 green-clad Jets fans to a city that truly hates New Yorkers. It seems to me that the people of Colorado despise everything about us, so it was almost fun listening to the heated verbal abuse that went on all weekend. I am telling you, folks, these people have quite a passion for their Broncos. They paint their homes, their cars, their streetlights, their pets, and even their kids Bronco Orange. But hey, what else do these people have? Mountains and rodeos? What happens in a New York minute takes twenty-four hours in Colorado.

Although I am very proud to be a New Yorker, I just could not get myself to root for the Jets. To me it's like a die-hard Yankee fan rooting for the Mets, or a Rangers fan rooting for the Islanders. It's just something that is taboo. You either embrace one or the other, not both. So imagine my dilemma when I was asked by the "Big Cheese Boss" to wear a Jets hat. This is where I drew the line. There is not enough fame or money at stake to get me to wear Jets green, and I am very proud of the fact that I didn't.

It comes down to principles, and I am a man who will stand by his principles to the bitter end. To me, being with a bunch of Jets fans was bad enough, but no one, and I mean no one, will ever make me root for them. I do give credit where it is due, and I admit they are a good football team. How can they not be? They have all ex-Giants coaching and playing for them, but I will not, and cannot, root for them. My Blue blood runs too deep, and the best thing about me is my loyalty. Whether to my teams or to my family and friends, I am as stubbornly loyal as they come. So take it for what it's worth, but no matter what the consequences, I root only for my teams.

Photo by Mike Malarkey

Monday Night Madness

It was a rare Monday night game at Giants stadium. We had planned for a classic Monster Tailgate party and arrived at the stadium at five o'clock. Little did we know that one of our boneheaded friends left his ticket at his girlfriend's house. The only man for the job was yours truly, the Pizza Man. We made it from the stadium to Staten Island and back in forty-seven minutes flat, just in time to enjoy our feast, which had been prepared while we were dodging traffic like men on a mission. Hey, after all, we *were* on a mission, and there was a lot of food to eat and a great football game to be played in a few hours. What topped off the whole night was watching the G-Men paste the Vikings in a nationally televised contest.

Photo by Seth Dinnerman

Pass the Pasta

Photo by Seth Dinnerman

Photo by Linda Kosarin

Pasta

Left Tackle Lasagna

1 pound ground beef
1/4 cup seasoned bread crumbs
1 egg, lightly beaten
Salt and pepper to taste
1 jar (2 pounds, 13 ounces to 3 pounds marinara sauce or Mariano's Marinara Sauce (page 128)
1 box (16 ounces) lasagna noodles
1 package (16 ounces) mozzarella cheese, cut into small cubes or shredded
1/2 cup grated Parmesan cheese

At home: Grease 13 x 9-inch baking pan; set aside. In bowl mix ground beef, bread crumbs, egg, salt, and pepper until well combined. Form into 3/4 to 1-inch meatballs. In large skillet cook until lightly browned. In large saucepan over medium-high heat combine marinara sauce and browned meatballs; bring to a boil. Reduce heat to low; cover and simmer 30 minutes. Meanwhile, cook lasagna noodles according to package directions. Drain. In prepared pan spoon in enough sauce to cover bottom. Top with 3 noodles placed lengthwise, then 1/3 ricotta cheese, 1/4 meatballs and sauce, and 1/4 mozzarella cheese. Place next layer noodles in opposite direction to cover. Repeat with 1/3 ricotta, 1/4 meatballs and sauce, and 1/4 mozzarella cheese. Repeat, ending with a layer of noodles topped with sauce, mozzarella, and Parmesan cheese. Bake in 350° F oven 1 to 1 1/4 hours or until hot and cheese melts.

At the game: Cut into serving pieces. Makes 8 to 10 servings.

Tailgate tip: Bake just before leaving for the game. Wrap tightly in foil and carry in insulated bag.

Here's a meal that has no equal,
Only a home team victory can be its sequel.
One that seems to have a lot of preparation,
But I'm sure your guests will stay for the duration.

The Pot

This is the story of "The Pot." Without The Pot, our parties would never be a success. It is because of this Pot that we as a crew enter every game intoxicated. There is no better feeling in the world. The smell in the parking lot from our Pot is like no other aroma your nose will ever smell. The best part about this pot is that it is perfectly legal.

Some of you are asking yourselves, "What is he talking about? Some pot at every game that seems to be worshiped as if it's the Holy Grail?" Well, it *is* our Holy Grail, and if you knew what The Pot does to us before each game, you would worship it too. You have to understand that fellow tailgaters wait with the anticipation of six-year-olds on Christmas Eve for us to show up with The Pot. Before The Pot is even taken out of the car, a crowd usually forms around us. As we unveil it, they cheer as if we'd already played the game and won. The gleam in the crowd's eyes is that of someone witnessing the Second Coming. They know they are in for something that will not only taste good going down, but will remain with them for the rest of their lives. Or at least until the next home game.

Photo by Mike Malarkey

Here's the story. My brother-in-law, Ralph, enjoys nothing more than sitting down to a great home-cooked meal, especially if it's prepared by my sister. Well, it was back in the early days and it was Ralph's first year as a season-ticket holder. It was Ralph's turn to provide our tailgate with the main course (we usually plan ahead, alternating who brings what and when).

At this particular point in Ralph's life, he had three young sons at home and was working three jobs. When Sunday morning came around and it was time to pack his car, he realized he had forgotten to go to the store and get the food for our feast.

Thank the Lord that my sister believes strongly in family values and tradition. As a good Italian, she had already fried eighty meatballs, which is a normal Sunday in their house, and had them simmering on the stove. The always quick-thinking and good-hearted Ralph saw his salvation and decided to take the meatballs to the game. He really had no choice, but that's besides the point. All he had to do on the way to the stadium was pick up a few loaves of Italian bread. Needless to say, we spent the rest of the day eating homemade meatball heros. Not only did we crush the hated Cowboys—the only other time we'd done that at home was in 1970—but it was the day the legend of The Pot was born. With its broken left handle and no handle on the lid, The Pot made its debut on November 9, 1980, the day our lousy football team broke an eight-game losing streak. I should also mention that the following week we brought The Pot and we beat the Packers! From then on, The Pot became our lucky charm. I know you might think that The Pot had nothing to do with those victories, but, hey, they were our only two wins in 1980 at home, in a year when we went 4–12.

Say what you will about our crazy rituals, but if you had seen and tasted what has been in The Pot over the years, you would understand. The Pot will be passed down for generations to come so our descendants can experience what it is like to be the owners of a very special Holy Grail, The Pot.

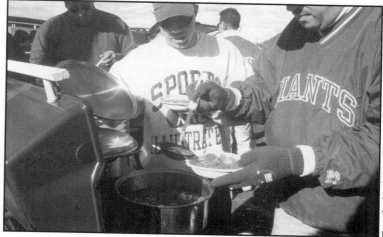

Photo by Linda Kosarin

Pasta

Linebacker Linguine

2 boxes (16 ounces each) linguine
4 tablespoons olive or other vegetable oil, divided
3 red bell peppers, cut into julienne strips
1 large onion, thinly sliced
3 medium carrots, cut into julienne strips
3 medium zucchini, cut into julienne strips
1/2 cup lemon juice
1/4 cup white wine
2 pounds jumbo shrimp, peeled and deveined

At home: Cook linguine according to package directions. Drain and toss with 2 tablespoons oil. Cool and place in flame-proof saucepan or Dutch oven. In large skillet or wok over medium heat in remaining hot oil cook red peppers and onion 2 minutes, stirring. Add carrots; cook 2 minutes or until tender. Add zucchini; cook 1 minute more. Add wine and lemon juice. Add vegetable mixture to pasta; toss to mix well. Cover tightly.

At the game: Preheat grill to medium heat. Place saucepan on grill. Heat linguine until hot, stirring occasionally. Place shrimp on grill. Cook 4 to 5 minutes or until pink, turning once. Add to pasta mixture. Makes 8 servings.

Tailgate tip: To cook shrimp without grilling, prepare vegetables as above. Remove vegetables from skillet and set aside. Add shrimp to pan juices in same skillet; cook 1 to 2 minutes until just pink. Return vegetables to skillet. Cook, stirring occasionally, until shrimp are pink. Add shrimp-vegetable mixture to linguine; toss to mix well.

It's what our linebackers like to do,
To quarterbacks not in blue.
A great way to carbo-up for a game,
It's also a great way to keep your crew tame.

Pasta

Pasta e Fagioli (or Pass the Fazool)

4 tablespoons olive or other vegetable oil
4 cloves garlic, crushed
2 ribs celery, finely chopped
6 ounces pepperoni, sliced 1/2-inch thick
2 cans (16 ounces each) white kidney beans (cannelloni beans)
1 can (10 1/4 to 13 3/4 ounces) ready-to-serve chicken broth
1/2 to 1 teaspoon dried oregano
Salt and pepper to taste
1 box (16 ounces) small pasta (such as diatali or ditalini), cooked
Grated Parmesan cheese, if desired

At home: In large saucepan over medium heat cook garlic and celery 2 minutes in hot oil. Add pepperoni; cook 3 to 5 minutes, stirring occasionally. Add beans, chicken broth, 1 1/2 cups water, oregano, and salt and pepper to taste. Bring to a boil. Reduce heat to low; cover and cook 30 minutes, stirring occasionally. Place in large thermos or in container in insulated bag. Place pasta in container or plastic bag, cover or seal tightly.

At the game: In large bowl toss hot bean-pepperoni mixture with pasta. Serve topped with cheese.

Tailgate tip: To round out the meal, serve with a green salad and Italian bread.

Here's a dish that stands alone,
Wherever you enjoy it, it reminds you of home.
No matter your color, religion, or creed,
Plenty of beer or wine to wash it down is all you'll need.

Attack of the Vikings

It has been quite some time since that debacle on December 27, 1996, the day we were invaded by Vikings disguised as a football team, the day that all Giants fans thought would be a showdown in Cheese Country. One minute and thirty seconds away from victory, and our Titanic dreams of an adventure in 1997 hit a purple iceberg and sank the hearts of all that bleed Blue.

I really cannot believe so much time has passed. The pain is still so fresh in my mind, as I'm sure it is in all of yours. A team that did not belong on the same field as our NFC East Champs made two plays and were given another, stealing what should have been a great win for us. I still cannot believe that I did not get to go to Lambeau Field with my Giants cheese grater to do battle with the mighty Packers. The impact and bitterness of that loss will never subside, but our hearts must go on. We will be back.

As the 1998 season got closer, the war cry was, "We have unfinished business!" It reminds me now of that dreaded 1985 ending we had in Chicago. Although the games ended a lot differently, the dejection and embarrassment was the same. We hoped that the bitter lessons learned in 1996 would carry over into the 1997–98 season and help the youngest team in football mature. We hoped that the new season would mirror 1986, when we went to the Big Dance and

Photo by Seth Dinnerman

120

took home the Queen. Unfortunately, an unsettled offensive line beset with injuries, a much tougher schedule, and some shaky play at quarterback put a damper on a season filled with such promise. Don't get me wrong, no one could have predicted the dream season we had in 1996, not even this always-optimistic Giants fan. To the team's credit, they stepped up in the second half of the 1997–98 season and finished at 8–8.

We Giants fans look forward to a very tough but promising season in 1999. No matter what the outcome, we, like no other fans in the league, will stand behind our team. With the leadership of our coach and his staff of dedicated assistants, the future looks nothing short of super. As you know, we are the fans that bleed Blue, and are never one to jump on any bandwagon. So I say this to our team as they prepare for a new season: "No matter what, at the season opener, the Meadowlands will be packed, and we fans will be with you every step of the way."

Photo by Seth Dinnerman

Gumbos, Stews, Chilis, & Sauces

Photo by Seth Dinnerman

Photo by Linda Kosarin

Soups & Stews

Goal Line Gumbo

1/2 cup vegetable oil, divided
3 pounds Italian sausage, cut into serving pieces
2 broiler-fryer chickens (about 2 1/2 pounds), cut into serving pieces
2 pounds jumbo shrimp, peeled and deveined
1/2 cup all-purpose flour
2 1/2 quarts chicken broth
1 large onion, chopped
1 red bell pepper, seeded and chopped
3 ribs celery, chopped
1 1/2 teaspoons liquid hot pepper sauce
1 1/2 teaspoons Worcestershire sauce
8 cups hot cooked brown rice

At home: *In large skillet over medium heat brown sausage in 2 tablespoons hot oil, turning occasionally. Remove and set aside. In same skillet add 2 tablespoons oil and chicken. Cook until golden brown, turning occasionally. Remove and set aside. To same skillet add shrimp. Cook 2 minutes until no longer pink. Remove and set aside. Add remaining oil to pan drippings in skillet. Stir in flour; cook, stirring, until lightly browned. Stir in chicken broth. Pour into saucepot. Add onion, pepper, celery, hot pepper sauce, and Worcestershire sauce. Bring to a boil. Reduce heat to low; cover and cook 40 minutes, stirring occasionally. Add sausage, chicken and shrimp. Cook 15 to 20 minutes more or until thickened and chicken is cooked through. Place in container in insulated bag.*

At the game: *Reheat if needed. Serve over brown rice. Makes 8 to 10 servings.*

Tailgate tip: *Bringing gumbo in a pot saves storing leftovers in another container and eases cleanup.*

> This dish is not for those who fear,
> Because as you eat it, I guarantee tears.
> Great for the days when the weather bites like a gator,
> But if you eat to much, you'll pay for it later.

Soups & Stews

Gridiron Gravy

3 to 5 pounds boneless venison meat, cut into 1-inch cubes
1 cup all-purpose flour
Salt and pepper to taste
1/4 cup vegetable oil
1 large Spanish or other sweet onion, thinly sliced
6 to 8 large carrots, peeled and cut into pieces
6 to 8 medium potatoes, peeled if desired and cut into pieces
4 ribs celery, cut into pieces
4 cups water
2 tablespoons liquid brown gravy enhancer

At home: Coat meat with mixture of flour, salt, and pepper. In large saucepan over medium-high heat brown meat and onions in hot oil, stirring occasionally, until evenly browned. Add water and gravy enhancer, scraping bottom to get up browned bits. Bring to a boil. Reduce heat to low; add vegetables. Cover and cook 2 hours or until meat and vegetables are tender.

At the game: Reheat if needed. Makes 8 to 12 servings.

Tailgate tip: This can be made at least a day ahead. Bring hot ready to eat or reheat on grill.

Another great meal to warm up your crew,
A dish that I like to call "Pizza Man Stew."
Eat hearty, my friends, and enjoy good health,
If you eat too much, just loosen that belt.

Soups & Stews

Chef Don Pintabona's Tribeca Grill Buffalo Chili

3 pounds boneless buffalo meat, cut into 1/2-inch cubes
2 pounds boneless beef chuck, cut into 1/2-inch cubes
2 to 4 tablespoons red chili powder
1/2 cup vegetable oil
4 to 6 medium white onions, coarsely chopped
2 to 6 cloves garlic, crushed
4 cups beef stock or bouillon
1 can (26 ounces) whole tomatoes, chopped
6 sprigs fresh tarragon
3 sprigs fresh rosemary
1 tablespoon dried oregano
1/3 cup creamy peanut butter
1/4 cup cocoa powder
Salt and pepper to taste

At home: In large storage container or plastic bag combine buffalo meat, beef, and red chili powder. Cover and refrigerate overnight. In large saucepan over medium heat in hot oil add onion and garlic. Cook, stirring, 5 minutes or until onion is tender. In same saucepan brown meat in batches. Return all meat to saucepan; add beef stock and tomatoes. Tie tarragon and rosemary into bundle; add with oregano to saucepan. Bring to a boil. Cover tightly and bake in 325° F oven 2 hours or until meat is tender, stirring every 30 minutes. Place saucepan on stove over low heat; stir in peanut butter and cocoa powder. Season with salt and pepper to taste.

At the game: Reheat if needed. Makes 12 to 15 servings.

Tailgate tip: Serve the chili over rice with crusty bread or rolls. If desired, use all beef or combination beef and pork.

Sauces

Mariano's Marinara Sauce with Meatballs

3 tablespoons olive or other vegetable oil
1/2 large onion, chopped
1 can (28 ounces) crushed tomatoes
1/2 cup red wine
Meatballs (recipe below)
1 teaspoon dried oregano
1 teaspoon dried basil

At home: In large saucepan over medium-high heat cook onions in hot oil, stirring occasionally, until tender. Add tomatoes, wine, and meatballs. Bring to a boil. Reduce heat to low; cover and cook 1 hour. Add oregano and basil. Cook, uncovered, until of desired consistency. Makes 4 to 6 servings.

Meatballs:
In large bowl mix until well combined:
1 pound ground beef
1 cup dried bread crumbs
2 eggs
1/4 cup white wine
2 cloves garlic, minced
1 teaspoon dried parsley
1 teaspoon grated Parmesan cheese

In large skillet in several tablespoons vegetable oil, cook in batches until evenly browned.

Tailgate tip: Great do-ahead item. Can be made months ahead of time and stored in freezer.

Sauces

Defensive Drippings

Drippings are various marinades for your barbecue meat recipes. It's best to marinate your meats overnight and use reserve marinade to brush on while meat is cooking on grill.

Running Back Rib Sauce

1/2 cup brown sugar
2/3 cup beef broth bouillon
2/3 cup Worcestershire sauce
3/4 cup granulated sugar
1 quart hot water
1 1/3 cups tomato paste

At home: In a large saucepan mix the sugar, beef broth, and water. Cook until all the sugar is dissolved. Add remaining ingredients and cook uncovered under low heat for 2 hours.

The Most Magical Season

The most magical season in Giants history was 1986. It was not only the year that Big Blue dominated the National Football League and won the Super Bowl, it was the sophomore year of the infamous chicken and the potato knish. My brother Tony and his lifelong friend Johnny Sarlo had unveiled the rubber chicken. (See page 93 for the story behind the hatching of the famous chicken.) This chicken, when waved frantically to the crowd, according to my brother and his buddy, was the reason why the Giants became competitive and, subsequently, champions. (These are grown men we're talking about here.) The first game the chicken took flight in my brother's arms, the Giants shut out the Philadelphia Eagles to start what would be a season of firsts.

My brother and Johnny also sat next to some guys who thought that a potato knish was the reason for such a good season. Talk about your rituals—these guys actually built little boxes to protect their magical treasures. They firmly believe to this day that the rubber chicken and the green-molded magic knish are the sole reasons why we won Super Bowl XXI. They make a valid point when they explain that the reason we got shut out in the playoffs against Chicago was because Johnny showed up at my brother's that day to watch the game, and had forgotten the chicken. Don't worry, folks, every time I see Johnny I let him know it was all his fault.

A Shattered Super Bowl Dream

It was January of 1986, and our team was preparing to go to Super Bowl XXI in Pasadena. This was the moment I had been waiting for all my life, and of course I was planning to go. But there was one small dilemma I had to deal with first. My significant other had just survived nine hours of spinal surgery. Would it be OK to leave her at home? I didn't really have to stay home and hold her hand, did I? She was recovering rather well, and the doctors said she would be up and about in no time at all. After all, it had been three whole days since the surgery. I can remember lying there in the middle of the night and thinking of every excuse possible to justify my going to sunny California in January and leaving my wife home and bedridden. "Why can't her family understand that we're in the Super Bowl?" I thought.

It soon became obvious that fate had made other plans. It seemed that I was destined to stay home and take care of my new bride. You know the deal, "For richer or poorer, in sickness and in health, till blah, blah, blah." Well, lo and behold, this is what happened, and believe it or not a very popular phrase everyone knows today was coined.

My lovely wife decided she needed a glass of milk, so being the caring and compassionate husband I am, I said sure. While feeling my way down the stairs in the dark, I went head over heels, catching my foot in the railing of the stairs and landing right on my head. Now, the landing on my head part was fine; the real problem was that I broke

Photo by Al Pereira

my foot and leg in six places. I was rushed to the hospital and put in traction for a week.

Needless to say, I didn't make the trip to Pasadena to see our beloved Giants whip the Broncos in Super Bowl XXI. I guess the lesson to be learned from this is there are more important things in life than the New York Football Giants, although I really can't think of any. (Please don't tell my wife I said that.) One other thing, about the phrase I mentioned. Whenever my family and friends see me now they ask, "Got milk?" You think that maybe the dairy farmers owe me something?

Photo by Seth Dinnerman

132

Snacks & Sides

Snacks & Sides

Grilled Pizza

1 package (16 ounces) mozzarella cheese
Assorted toppings: sliced peppers, thin onion wedges, thinly sliced pepperoni, anchovies, sliced meatballs, etc.
12 pita breads (4- to 6-inches each)
1 jar (26 ounces) spaghetti sauce (about 3 cups)

At home: Shred mozzarella cheese, wrap tightly. Prepare desired toppings, wrap tightly.

At the game: Preheat grill to medium heat. Place pitas on grill. Cook until lightly toasted and heated through. Turn; top generously with sauce, shredded cheese, and desired toppings. Cook until cheese is melted and toppings hot. Makes 12 servings.

This one's my favorite, as you might have guessed,
Another great dish that can make quite a mess.
The secret is to be free, to let go and create,
Because the more on your pizza, the more on your plate.

Snacks & Sides

Grilled Vegetables

Assorted vegetables:
Asparagus, tough stems removed
Small carrots, trimmed and peeled
Eggplant, ends trimmed, sliced crosswise 1/2-inch thick
Bell peppers, stems removed, seeded and cut into 1-inch pieces
New potatoes, cut in half
Zucchini or yellow squash, trimmed, cut into lengthwise strips
Olive or other vegetable oil, melted butter or margarine

At home: In saucepan over high heat bring small amount of water to boil. Tie 3 to 4 asparagus spears in bundle with blanched green onion tops, add to saucepan, cook 2 minutes. Add carrots, cook 3 to 5 minutes. Add potatoes, cook 10 minutes. Drain well. Cool slightly; place in storage container and cover tightly.

At the game: Preheat grill to medium heat. Brush grill with oil to prevent vegetables from sticking. Brush vegetables with oil, butter, or margarine. Place on grill. Cook asparagus 3 to 5 minutes; carrots, 3 to 5 minutes; eggplant, 6 to 8 minutes; bell peppers, 8 to 10 minutes; potatoes, 10 to 12 minutes; squash, 6 to 8 minutes.

The Mistake

At a very early age I found out exactly how sacred New York Football Giants season tickets were to my father. My mother, bless her heart, had done the unthinkable. Without checking, she inadvertently threw out an envelope containing—you guessed it—three sets of Giants season tickets. I don't think I have ever seen my dad more disturbed. After Dad blew steam for a while and continued to remind Mom of what a mistake she had made, he left the house and began a systematic garbage can search for the missing tickets. The scene was straight out of an "I Love Lucy" routine, with my Dad going from garbage can to garbage can, scouring through dirty diapers, coffee grounds, and numerous other funky garbage while my grandmother chased him around the block trying to get him back in the house. Meanwhile, Mom, ever the cool, calm, and collected woman, made one phone call to the Giants and straightened the whole thing out. Needless to say, Dad got his tickets, and we knew from that day forward that Mom and Dad would stay together forever.

Photo by Seth Dinnerman

Snacks & Sides

Potato Pie

Dry bread crumbs to taste
5 medium all-purpose potatoes, peeled and cut into pieces
1 1/2 cup milk
1 egg, lightly beaten
1/2 package (8 ounces) mozzarella cheese, shredded or diced (4 ounces)
2 tablespoons grated Parmesan cheese
5 tablespoons butter or margarine, divided
2 tablespoons chopped, fresh or 1 tablespoon dried parsley
Salt and pepper to taste

At home: Grease 9-inch pie pan; sprinkle with bread crumbs and set aside. In large saucepan over high heat in 1-inch water place potatoes. Bring to a boil. Cover and cook 15 to 20 minutes or until tender. Drain well. Preheat oven to 350° F. In large bowl with mixer or masher, mash potatoes. Add milk, egg, mozzarella cheese, 3 tablespoons butter, Parmesan cheese, and parsley; mix until well combined. Season with salt and pepper. Spoon into prepared pie plate. Sprinkle top with additional bread crumbs and dot with remaining 2 tablespoons butter. Bake 30 minutes or until lightly browned. Wrap tightly in foil; place in insulated bag.

At the game: Unwrap and spoon out to serve. Makes 4 to 6 servings.

Tailgate tip: Bake the day before and reheat on the grill, or prepare up to baking, place in flame-proof casserole and cook on covered grill until heated through at the game.

Snacks & Sides

Mama Frizalone's Spaghetti Pie

Mama Frizalone is the mother-in-law of my editor, John Rutledge. This is a really great dish and I am happy to include it. If I didn't, JR told me Mama Friz would give me the sign of the horns!

> 1 pound spaghetti—cook according to package directions and set aside to cool.
> 1 dozen eggs
> 1/2 cup dried or fresh parsley
> 1 1/2 cups grated Romano cheese
> 2 cups sun dried tomatoes (cut in strips) in olive oil
> 2 cups cooked Italian sweet sausage, if desired
> Pepper to taste

At home: In a bowl combine all ingredients. Add cooked spaghetti to the mixture. Place mixture in a greased aluminum lasagna tin and bake for approximately one hour or until top is golden brown. Let cool and store in original tin for convenience.

At the game: Cut into 2-inch squares and mangia, enjoy!

Snacks & Sides

Field Goal Fries

8 large all-purpose potatoes, peeled if desired
1/4 cup butter or margarine, cut into pieces
Ground paprika to taste
Salt and pepper to taste

At home: In large saucepan over high heat in 1-inch water place potatoes. Bring to a boil. Cover and cook 10 to 15 minutes or until just fork tender. Drain. Cool slightly; cut into 1/2-inch slices or wedges. On large sheet of heavy duty foil place potatoes. Top with butter, paprika, salt, and pepper. Wrap tightly.

At the game: Preheat grill to medium heat. Place foil packet with potatoes on grill. Cook 20 to 30 minutes or until hot.

Tailgate tip: Carefully move and remove the foil packet with rounded tongs so foil doesn't tear and butter pour out and flame.

Snacks & Sides

Special Teams Salsa

2 medium tomatoes, coarsely chopped
2 large green onions, coarsely chopped
2 cloves garlic, minced
4 tablespoons tomato paste
1 tablespoon lemon juice
1 tablespoon olive oil or other vegetable oil
Salt and pepper to taste
Taco or nacho chips

At home: In large jar or container combine tomatoes, green onions, garlic, tomato paste, lemon juice, oil, salt, and pepper until well mixed. Cover and refrigerate.

At the game: Place in serving bowl and serve with chips.

Tailgate tip: This salsa can double as an appetizer as well as a sauce over hamburgers, steak, fish, or chicken.

Snacks & Sides

Mary's Serious Shepherd's Pie

1 9-inch prepared pie crust
12 small, all-purpose potatoes, peeled
1 pound ground lamb or beef
4 tablespoons butter or margarine
1/3 cup of milk
1/2 package (8 ounces) mozzarella cheese, shredded or diced (4 ounces)
1 jar (6 ounces) ready-to-use beef gravy
1 package (10 ounces) frozen peas and carrots, thawed

At home: In 9-inch pie plate place pie crust and flute edges if desired; set aside. In large saucepan over high heat place potatoes in 1 inch water. Bring to a boil. Cover and cook 15 to 20 minutes or until tender. Meanwhile, in medium skillet over medium heat cook lamb or beef until well browned, stirring occasionally. Drain well and set aside. Preheat oven to 375° F. Drain potatoes well. In large bowl with mixer or masher, mash potatoes. Add milk and butter until smooth. Stir in mozzarella cheese. In prepared pie crust place 1/2 potato mixture; top evenly with cooked lamb or beef and peas and carrots. Pour in gravy over meat and vegetables. Spoon on remaining potato mixture to form peaks. Bake 45 minutes or until heated through and top is browned. Wrap tightly in foil; place in insulated bag.

At the game: Unwrap and spoon out to serve. Makes 6 to 7 servings.

Tailgate tip: If you enjoy chilled or room temperature potatoes, make a day ahead of time and serve cut in wedges at the game.

Snacks & Sides

Playoff Prosciutto and Melon

1 large (2 pounds) honeydew melon, seeded and cut into quarters
12 thin slices prosciutto, cut in half lengthwise
24 toothpicks

At home: Remove rind from melon quarters and cut each quarter into 6 pieces, making 24 pieces. Wrap a strip of prosciutto around each melon piece and secure with toothpick. Place in container; cover and seal tightly.

At the game: Uncover and enjoy!

Tailgate tip: If you don't have time to do this in advance, bring a sharp knife and do it in minutes at the game.

Snacks & Sides

Home Team Hot Wings

12 chicken wings
3/4 cup honey
3/4 cup soy sauce
Juice of two lemons (about 4 tablespoons)
1 clove garlic, minced
1 tablespoon Worcestershire sauce
1 to 3 teaspoons liquid hot pepper sauce to taste

At home: Preheat oven to 325° F. Cut tips from chicken wings; cut wings in two at joint. Place in single layer in shallow baking pan.

To make sauce: In bowl mix remaining ingredients until well combined; brush over chicken wings. Bake 45 to 60 minutes or until cooked through and brown, turning occasionally and brushing with sauce. Place in tightly-covered container; place in insulated bag.

At the game: Uncover and enjoy! Makes 8 to 10 servings.

Tailgate tip: If desired, wings can be made up two days ahead of time and reheated or served at room temperature.

Snacks & Sides

Halftime Ham Rolls

1 package (3 ounces) cream cheese, at room temperature
2 tablespoons lemon juice
2 tablespoons mayonnaise
1 teaspoon fresh or 1/2 teaspoon dried parsley
1 teaspoon finely minced onion
8 slices (about 1/2 to 1 ounce each) smoked ham

At home: In blender or food processor place cream cheese, lemon juice, mayonnaise, parsley, and onion; process until smooth. Spread 1/8 cheese mixture evenly over each slice of ham; roll up tightly. Cut into bite-sized pieces. Place in plastic container. Cover tightly and refrigerate.

At the game: Stick each with a toothpick and enjoy! Makes 8 to 10 servings.

Tailgate tip: Vary the filling by adding a bit of mustard, different herbs (thyme, oregano), or a drop of hot pepper sauce.

It's President "Pizza Man" to you, Pal!

I am living a dream most fans would love to live. I've been able to go to all the Giants' away games with the ultimate road trip company, Big Blue Travel. I was once told by a very dear friend of mine, who now roots for his team from heaven, that I would leave my impression on the world in a very big way. Well, besides having been blessed with three beautiful angels to nurture and raise, I have been blessed also with the greatest part-time job in the world.

In a different city on any given week, I get to lead a group of the best sports fans on a fun-filled weekend. I get to chaperone these great fans to wonderful cocktail parties in the best hotels each city has to offer, and on game day I get to host the best tailgate party money can buy. Then, of course, I get to go to the game in the unfriendly confines of an enemy stadium. All this, and I get compensated, too. I know, unbelievable, right? Please don't hate me for saying this, but it's a tough job and somebody has to do it.

Photo by Seth Dinnerman

I'm sorry, folks, but you have to understand. This Pizza Guy is just living the life of a jetsetter (well, almost; I do have Cadillac tastes with Hyundai pockets). One weekend I'm in sunny San Diego with a group of Yankees fans to watch our well-oiled team sweep the Padres. The next weekend, I may be in Texas to watch our beloved G-Men do battle with the hated Cowgirls. It's been quite a ride, and so far, the very best place I have been to date is our nation's capital.

Halloween in Georgetown was an experience not soon to be forgotten. Let me set the stage for you. Big Blue Travel's annual trip was hosted by the Commander-in-Chief himself, Mr. William Clinton. Well, it wasn't really him, but my first name is William, so you figure it out. I donned a $500 suit and a Clinton mask. While standing on a corner in Georgetown, with hundreds of people all decked out in their best Halloween costumes, this Pizza Dude was at his political best, campaigning on Mr. Clinton's behalf. As the crowds ebbed and flowed around me, I would raise my arms and speak for all to hear, "I did not touch that woman," "I had my eyes closed the whole time," "I'm sorry my fellow Americans," "It was all Hillary's fault."

It was quite a hoot, and judging by the reactions of everyone who was there, a good time was had by all. It was the night that Bubba C. vindicated himself in the city that loves him so dearly. I'm telling you, folks, I had people lining up to shake their hero's hand, and a few even slipped me—him—a few coins. Please don't tell Bill's lawyers though; he may be charged back taxes on it. I have to be honest though, the rest of the night was kind of a blur. It must have been because the cigar I was smoking all night melted my mask and I couldn't see through the eye holes anymore. The Irish whiskey I had with dinner helped a little, too, I guess. Good clean fun—that's what it's all about, folks.

Photo by Seth Dinnerman

147

Salads

Photo by Seth Dinnerman

Photo by Seth Dinnerman

Photo by Seth Dinnerman

Salads

Right Tackle Taco Salad

1 package (6 to 8 ounces) taco seasoning
1 pound chopped meat
1 package (4 to 6 ounces) cheddar cheese
8 tomatoes, diced
1 quart sour cream
1 head of lettuce, shredded

At home: Brown chopped meat in fry pan. Drain. Add taco seasoning and 1 cup of water. Stir over medium heat until thick. Let cool. When meat is cool, spread evenly in a deep pasta-serving dish. Spread sour cream on top of seasoned meat. Add strips of lettuce, diced tomatoes, and shredded cheddar cheese. Make sure to cover all the sour cream. Chill overnight. Bring to tailgate with nacho chips.

Another one you prepare at home,
Far from the table you should not roam.
'Cause if you do I'm sure you'll see,
A tasty treat that used to be.

Salads

Super Bowl Salad

2 cups small fresh broccoli spears
2 tablespoons red wine vinegar
4 cups fresh torn spinach
2 tablespoons balsamic vinegar
2 sliced onions
2 tablespoons honey
2 cups mushrooms, sliced
3 tablespoons olive oil
Salt and pepper to taste

At home: Cook broccoli until tender and bright green. Chill. Toss spinach, mushrooms, onion, and broccoli. Whisk together olive oil, vinegars, honey, salt, and pepper. Pour vinaigrette over veggies to coat. Pack in container and place in cooler. Serves 4 to 6.

Salads

Momma Cross's Potato Salad

Howard Cross — (TE) Alabama. Drafted in sixth round in 1989. With Giants from 1989 to present. A fierce blocker with good hands, Howard is a vital part of the Giants offense. Howard's mom was gracious in providing me with her recipe for her down-home potato salad. Enjoy!

10 medium all-purpose potatoes, peeled and cut into cubes
1/2 to 1 cup light mayonnaise
3 tablespoons prepared mustard
2 to 3 tablespoons sweet pickle relish
1 large onion, finely chopped
Salt and pepper to taste

At home: In large saucepot over high heat place potatoes in 1 inch water. Bring to a boil. Cover and cook 10 to 15 minutes or until just fork-tender. Drain well. In large storage container or bowl mix mayonnaise, mustard, relish, and onion until well combined. Add potatoes; toss until well coated. Season with salt and pepper. Cover tightly and refrigerate.

At the game: Uncover and enjoy.

Tailgate tip: This salad tastes even better when made a day ahead and refrigerated overnight.

Salads

My Mary's Italian Macaroni Salad

My Mary is my driving force, my wife for fourteen years, and the mother of my three little angels. Her strength and determination are enough to inspire anyone. This and her macaroni salad are what keep me reaching for my dreams, no matter how unreachable they may seem.

1 1/2 pounds tri-color fusili macaroni (corkscrew)
1 8-ounce bottle Italian dressing
1/2 pound prosciutto (Italian ham), cubed
1/2 pound mozzarella cheese, cubed
1/2 pound provolone cheese, cubed
1 can black olives
3 plum tomatoes, diced
3 stalks celery, diced
1 carrot, grated

At home: Cook macaroni according to package directions. Let cool. Place in a large serving bowl, add all ingredients, and toss.

At the game: Enjoy!

It Isn't Always Easy Being Blue

It isn't always easy being a True-Blue Giants fan. I can still remember going to school on Mondays having to defend a team so ineffective that the networks wouldn't even televise the games. I guess it was out of fear of what people might do to their television sets. Oh, how times have changed!

I currently hold an unofficial record for missing only one home game since the Meadowlands opened in 1976 (my cousin chose to get married on opening day in 1991, breaking my streak). I vowed never again to let anything like that stop me. I also pride myself on being the guy who throws Monster Tailgate Parties. In those lean years, the tailgate was often better than the game. So we endured and stayed True-Blue, and were rewarded with two of the most unforgettable seasons, 1986 and 1990.

If you're looking for the fan of fans, you just need to walk out of the tunnel an hour before game time and look up in the stands. I will be there to boastfully greet you, as I do all visitors to our house. Just look for the guy with the Giants hard hat and an LT No. 56 or Pizza Man No. 1 jersey, pumping up his beloved Giants to do battle. One other thing: I have three favorite teams in the NFL—the Giants and whoever is playing the Jets and the hated Cowboys.

Photo by Mike Malarkey

155

Some Fun Football Definitions

The Draft: The NFL Draft Rule was adopted in 1936 as a way to allocate graduating college players in a fair manner to existing teams.

Free Agency: Free Agency came into being in 1992 as a result of a lawsuit filed in 1989 by the NFL Players Association. The players' union sued to provide NFL players with the freedom of movement between teams.

The Fumble

Dare I mention that infamous game with the Philadelphia Eagles and "The Fumble?" This Giant "lowlight " had to be the most often-shown clip on every football show across America. It also marked the last time this Giants fan (and I'm sure many others) would ever leave before the final gun again.

Just like three-fourths of the stadium that day, I too was in the parking lot celebrating a rare Giants victory before the end of regulation time. With less than two minutes to go, Joe Pisarcik handed off to Larry Czonka. It was a routine play, but the ball squirted loose, was picked up by the Eagles' Herman Edwards, and run in for a touchdown. The sounds we heard from the remaining fans who had stayed in the stadium still linger in my mind. First we heard the unnatural hush of the crowd, and then the incredibly loud booing throughout the Tri-State area. I, like all Giants fans, still struggle to erase this debacle from my memory.

Sweet Stuff

Photo by Seth Dinnerman

Photo by Seth Dinnerman

Dessert

Kitty Fassel's Monster Cookies

Kitty Fassel is the wife of Giants head coach Jim Fassel. Kitty has made these cookies for more than twenty-two years, spanning the ten different teams that coach Fassel has worked with. This recipe goes back to 1976 and was originally provided to Kitty by another coach's wife at the University of Utah. The monster cookies have a special place in Kitty's and Coach Fassel's history, as the recipe was given to Kitty during Coach Fassel's first real job in the business.

Photo by Linda Kosarin

16 cups old-fashioned oats
2 cups all-purpose flour
8 teaspoons baking soda
3 jars (1 pound each) creamy or crunchy peanut butter
1 pound margarine, softened
2 packages (16 ounces each) brown sugar
12 eggs
1 teaspoon vanilla extract
1 bag (16 ounces) semi-sweet chocolate chips
1 bag (16 ounces) candy-coated chocolate pieces

At home: Preheat oven to 325° F. In medium bowl stir oats, flour, and baking soda until well combined. In large bowl with mixer at medium speed beat peanut butter, margarine, and brown sugar until well combined. Beat in eggs, corn syrup, and vanilla extract. Stir in oat-flour mixture until well combined. Add chocolate chips and candy-coated chocolate pieces. On ungreased baking sheets, drop by rounded tablespoonfuls to form about 3-inch mounds. Bake 15 to 18 minutes or until lightly browned. Remove and cool on racks. Makes about 100 cookies.

At the game: Enjoy!

Tailgate tip: If you make them ahead of time, pack a dozen or two in plastic bags, seal, and freeze. It will take at least half a day to complete the baking.

NOTE: The large quantities necessary for the recipe may sound crazy until you realize the end result will make fifty hungry football players extremely satisfied.

Dessert

Kent "Graham Cracker" Pudding Cake (Old Fashioned Icebox Cake)

Kent Graham — (QB) Ohio State. Drafted in the eighth round (211th pick overall). With Giants from 1992 to 1994; waived on August 30, 1995; re-signed as a free agent on February 17, 1998. After taking over from Dave Brown in the middle of the season, Kent's leadership and a 5-1 performance helped turn a difficult season into a respectable 8-8. Kent reports to this year's camp as the incumbent starter at quarterback. Born November 1, 1968.

> 2 boxes chocolate pudding mix
> milk (as directed on pudding mix box)
> 1 box graham crackers
> 1 can whipped cream

Photo by Jim Turner

Prepare chocolate pudding according to box directions. Let cool. In a deep-dish pan, layer bottom with whole graham crackers. Add a layer of pudding, about half an inch, add another layer of whole graham crackers, then another layer of pudding. Repeat until pan is full, add a final layer of graham crackers, then refrigerate. Serve cold after topping with whipped cream.

> *This is one that my whole family loved,*
> *A simple treat that is far and above.*
> *Whenever I make it, it takes me back far,*
> *Because the first time I had it, it was from grandma.*

Dessert

Quarterback Crunch

2 boxes (5 ounces each) caramel popcorn
1 box (12 ounces) oven-toasted corn cereal
1 jar (12 ounces) honey-roasted peanuts
1 cup semi-sweet chocolate chips

At home: In large storage container or plastic bag combine all ingredients until well mixed.

At the game: Toss again to mix well. Serve in paper cups or napkins.

Tailgate tip: Always leave an extra roll of aluminum foil in your trunk to wrap up tailgate leftovers and bring them inside the stadium to munch.

The quarterback we love to crunch,
With this one, you're sure to munch.
If you don't enjoy it, what can I say,
You'll live to tailgate another day.

Dessert

Pizza Man's Chocolate Chip Cookies

1 cup plus 2 tablespoons all-purpose flour
1 teaspoon baking soda
1/2 teaspoon salt
1/2 cup firmly packed light brown sugar
6 tablespoons granulated sugar
1/2 cup (1 stick) lightly salted butter or margarine, softened
1 egg, beaten
1 teaspoon vanilla extract
1 package (6 ounces) semi-sweet chocolate chips
1 cup chopped walnuts

At home: Preheat oven to 375° F. In medium bowl stir flour, baking soda, and salt until well combined. In large bowl with mixer at medium speed beat sugars and butter until light and fluffy. Beat in egg and vanilla. Stir in flour mixture. Stir in chips and walnuts. On ungreased baking sheets, drop by rounded teaspoonfuls about 2 inches apart. Bake 10 to 15 minutes or until lightly browned. Let stand 1 minute. Remove and cool on racks. Makes about 4 dozen cookies.

At the game: Enjoy!

Tailgate tip: Freeze milk the night before and let thaw on the way to the game for cold milk to have with the cookies.

A "Giant" Yankee Fan

John Travolta to my right, Jerry Vale to my left. One row behind me was Tom Arnold, Michael Eisner, the Disney giant, and John Tish of Tish Construction. Three rows in front of me was "Mr. October," Reggie Jackson, and the ever-so-humble family of "Mr. Yankee," Roger Maris. Yes, folks, the stars were all out on this night, and the Pizza Dude was among them all.

It was October 21, 1998, in sunny San Diego, and the only stars worth writing about were the ones out there on the diamond. The most famous and storied franchise in all of sports was about to settle, once and for all, the debate over who the greatest team of all time really was.

You may be wondering why I am writing about this in a football book, but, hey, these are my beloved Yankees, and I was about to watch men dismantle little boys on their way to becoming the best of the best.

It was game four of the 1998 Fall Classic, and just as they did the entire season, the "Bronx Bombers" were about to rewrite the history books. It didn't matter that they won 116 games during the regular season. We had to win the big one to make this dream season reach the pinnacle.

Well, I guess I don't have to tell you true sports fans what happened next, but for the others . . . Our New York Yankees disposed of the Sandy Taco Padres in four straight games.

It wasn't enough drama that in game two at the house that Ruth built (and not Steinbrenner), Chuck Knoblauch would atoned for his brain-lock play in the American League Championship Series. He hit the biggest home run of his life to propel us to Qualcomm Stadium, up two games to none.

It also was not enough that in game three, "Mr. MVP" Scott Brosius would hit a mammoth shot off the best relief pitcher in baseball. No, "The Bombers" had some more drama to give us. I really wasn't sure how much more this little heart of mine could take, but I was ready for it. Andy Pettitte took the

Goal Posts: The Y–shaped structures located at the farthest end of each end zone. The horizontal crossbar is ten feet high, and the span between the uprights is eighteen feet, six inches. The vertical posts must extend at least thirty feet above the crossbar. A ribbon four inches wide by forty-two inches long must be attached to the top of each vertical post.

Hash Marks: Inbound lines that are seventy feet, nine inches from each sideline.

Regulation Size: Footballs must be 11 to 11.25 inches long and weigh 14 to 15 ounces. Thirty-six approved footballs, provided by the home team, are required for every game played outdoors, and twenty-four are required for games played indoors.

Officials: Each NFL game requires seven officials. Each official has specific duties and positions on the field.

Referee: The referee is the leader of the officials. He generally is positioned ten to twelve yards behind the offensive line of scrimmage. He usually follows the backfield action on running and pass plays and determines fouls such as illegal motions and forward progress, roughing the passer, fumbles, and incomplete passes.

mound and pitched a gem of a game, ultimately shutting down the Sorry Diego Padres and completing the four-game sweep.

The real drama took place the next day, watching all the diehard Yankees fans trying to get back to New York for the parade. The best mayor our city has ever had was thinking of himself again and not the fans. I say this with a warm heart because I respect and love what Rudy G. has done for our city, but what was he thinking? He scheduled the parade down the Canyon of Heroes only two days after we won.

You might be saying, "What's the big deal?" but to the five to ten thousand fans that made the trek to California, it was a major big deal. As most Yankees diehards scrambled to get home, I myself decided to enjoy a round of golf. Besides, I had to stay with the group I was leading for the Ultimate Road Trip Company, Big Blue Travel.

To me it really did not matter. I have been lucky enough to be part of countless parades down the Canyon of Heroes in my lifetime: for the Yankees (three times), the Rangers (in 1994), and even the real heroes of the world, the Desert Storm troops. So missing this one, although I would have loved to have been there, was no big deal. To some Yankees fans, it was like a life-or-death mission to get there, and I really did feel bad for those who didn't make it. But, hey, like I said when they showed me on ABC news that October night from Qualcomm Stadium with my Yankees hard hat on, "We came, we saw, we conquered in four!"

Gabrielle's First Game

It was Saturday, August 17, 1996, and our Giants were playing the forever tenants of the Meadowlands, the No-Town Jets. It was our annual preseason matchup that to the Jets is always like their Super Bowl. To us, of course, it is just another tune-up for the regular season, but this game was different. It was a monumental game in the life of the Pizza Man.

You see, it was my baby Gabrielle's very first New York Football Giants game. Well, maybe it wasn't her first, but it was the first one that she could understand. I can remember how excited Gabrielle was. She was all dressed in her Sunday football best: her Giants jersey, her Giants pants, and, of course, her Giants hard hat. The only problem was she was up and ready to go at 5:00 AM.

I remember how thrilled I was that my Gabrielle was going to experience her first professional football game. I also remember that I was very apprehensive. My sweet, innocent little angel was about to be exposed to her daddy's pregame ritual. Don't get me wrong, when I stand at the tunnel an hour before kickoff to let the opposition know that they're in for a giant battle, I do so without ever using profanity. After all, I do have a reputation to uphold and would never jeopardize the dignity of our storied franchise. I just do a lot of taunting, while exposing the non-athletes for what they are: big, fat monstrosities who pose as football players. You know the players I'm talking

Photo by Al Pereira

165

Umpire: Usually lines up four to five yards downfield. Looks for false starts and penalizes offensive and defensive linemen for contact infractions. He also assists on rulings of incomplete passes or trapped balls.

Head Linesman: Primarily responsible for actions on the line of scrimmage prior to and during the snap. With the referee, the linesman keeps track of the number of downs and is responsible for supervising the chain crew.

about—the ones who should be eating and drinking in the parking lot with the rest of us.

On this day, the usual crowd was waiting for me at the tunnel. They all got such a kick out of this cute little golden-haired cherub dressed from head to toe in Giants gear. That is, of course, until she heard what her daddy was saying to those hated Y-E-T-S. (I call them YETS because they ain't done nothing YET!)

Instead of being surprised or embarrassed like any seven year old would be of what her favorite Pizza Dude was saying, she just chimed right in. I would yell something to a Yets player, and she would either repeat it or add to it.

I will never forget the looks on the ex-Giants players' faces who were now playing for the Yets. Guys like Pepper Johnson, Leonard Marshall, Jumbo Elliot, and even Bill Parcells. They were looking at me, shaking their heads, and I'm sure they were saying to themselves, not only are we the enemies now and have to hear the wrath of the Pizza Man, but he has brought with him a squeaky, and just as loud, voice.

It was hilarious, and I don't believe I have ever felt more proud as a father, listening to my sweet little angel Gabrielle tongue-lash the opposition with the gusto of her old man. She did this with the utmost respect and determination any rabid football fan and father would be proud of. Of course, I might add, she used no profanity.

The Darling of the Meadowlands

It was December 13, 1998, a day that should go down in Giants history as a day when fans of the NFL would witness "The Mini-Miracle at the Meadowlands." It was a day that I will never forget as long as I live. A day when Dolphins fans everywhere became Giants fans for at least one game. A day when every Dolphins fan across America knew they would never be able to beat the undefeated Denver Broncos if the Giants didn't knock them off first.

A day that, when the game was over, allowed Dolphins fans to exhale such a collective gasp of relief through their blowholes that it could have caused a hurricane in sunny Miami.

On this day, the Giants proved that on any given Sunday, any team can beat another. Maybe it was the Giants as a team responding with pride to the fact that every newspaper columnist in the country had them in the loss column way before kickoff. Perhaps it was our talented coaching staff that came up with a game plan that stifled the highest-rated offense in football. Yet another reason could be that the best and most loyal fans in football showed up and made the Meadowlands an unfriendly place in which to play such an important game.

Photo by Linda Kosarin

These are all legitimate reasons for us shocking the Broncos. Now for the real reason the Giants stopped the Broncos' quest for an undefeated season . . .

On this most unforgettable day, something magical happened to a beautiful nine-year-old girl. I finally had another opportunity to take my little angel, Gabrielle, to see what her father is so passionate about on football Sundays. As always, we had a great tailgate party and went into the stadium an hour before kickoff. She could not wait to get to that tunnel where the players take the field and let those Broncos know that "the streak ends today," as she emphatically stated.

With the conviction of a daughter who learned at the feet of her daddy, she let all in earshot know that the pizza does not fall far from the oven.

I was so proud of my daughter. The sun was shining, the stadium was already buzzing with electricity, and you could almost smell an upset in the making. Things couldn't get much better.

Until, of course, what happened next.

Up from the field came one of the directors of marketing for the Giants, Bill Smith. He asked my Gabrielle if she would like to be the honorary Tee-Girl. Smith explained that the little boy who was scheduled for today was at home, sick. The Tee-Girl or Boy gets to go onto the field, and after the opening kickoff, runs out and retrieves the football tee.

Photo by Seth Dinnerman

I can't tell you who was more excited, my daughter Gabrielle or me. Not only was she about to be part of the history being made that day, but her Daddy was going to be on the field, too. You have to understand, folks, that to me, going onto the field is like a priest being chosen to say the gospel at the Vatican. I was on the sacred ground that all the

Giants greats, past and present, have bled and sweated on over the years.

Now of a nine year old you might say, "What does she know?" but this is no ordinary nine year old. This is my nine year old, and she fully understood how very special this was, to be "The Chosen One" . . . "The Tee-Girl." After watching the players being introduced from the field, it was time for kickoff. On the jumbo screen they showed my angel, donning Daddy's hard hat and wearing a smile as sweet as candy as they announced her name. She played the crowd like a seasoned veteran, waving and throwing kisses. Her Daddy was so proud, and a little envious.

It was kickoff time and all she could say to me was, "Daddy, these guys are really big. Now I know why they call them Giants." The coin toss was over, and the Giants would kick off. As the teams took the field I was trying to reassure her and give her some pointers. She turned to me and said, "Daddy, this is not rocket science. I can handle it. Relax, will ya!" (I told you she wasn't an ordinary nine year old. She really is an adult fan trapped inside a nine year old's body.)

Seventy-eight thousand people were about to watch my little angel run onto the field to pump up what would become a frenzied crowd. Being the daughter of the Pizza Man, she couldn't just run out there, pick up the tee, and run back. Not my Gabrielle, no way. She had a game plan of her own.

After the opening kickoff, in which the Giants set the tone by punishing Denver's return man, the stage was set.

My little angel trotted onto the field in pursuit of the tee. Her little feet were going a mile a minute, but to me she was going in slow motion. She reached the tee but instead of coming right back, she began to wave and blow kisses to all the Giants faithful. This was her big chance to shine, and boy, was she ever relishing the limelight. The crowd stood, cheered, waved, and threw kisses right back to her. Maybe it was just me, but I could not get over (and still can't) how this little nine year old was working this opportunity for all it was worth. When she got back to the sidelines, she leaped into my

Line Judge: Straddles the line of scrimmage on the side of the field opposite the head linesman. He, like the linesman, is also responsible for offside or encroachment calls. Remains at line of scrimmage during punts to determine if players, other than the end men, move downfield too quickly. Line judge also advises referee when time has expired in each quarter.

Back Judge: The back judge operates on the same side of the field as the line judge, but he is about twenty yards downfield. He rules on holding, pass interference, out-of-bounds, and assists the field judge in determining if field goals are good.

Side Judge: The side judge positions himself on the same side of the field as the line judge but is twenty yards deep. He rules on holding or illegal use of hands by offense and on defensive fouls. His primary responsibility is to make decisions regarding the sidelines on his side of the field, e.g., receiver or runner out-of-bounds. Also watches for clipping on punt returns, and acts as a double umpire on field goals and points after touchdown.

arms and said the words all daddies of little girls know and cherish so dearly, "You're the greatest daddy in the whole world and I love you." After wiping the tears from my eyes, she said one more thing that kept them flowing. "I'm going to sing the National Anthem on this field some day, daddy, and I'm gonna make everyone here say 'Whitney who?'"

So now you know. The real reason why the Giants won this monumental game was because of the "Little Darling of the Meadowlands." She not only wowed the crowd to their feet, but she vowed she'd be back. She helped set the tone for the rest of the game and never lost a step. The Bumbling Broncos still are trying to figure out what hit them. We can't tell them it was a nine year old, because they may never recover. As for that little angel of mine, she is hooked on the greatest game this side of paradise, and she may never come down off that cloud.

Daddy's Little Angels

I am probably the luckiest man on the face of the earth, not only because I have a spiritual angel on my shoulder and in my heart, but because I also am surrounded by real angels. Every day, I awake to hear their tiny voices saying: "Good morning, Daddy, where's my breakfast?" It is truly music to my ears when, while still in bed, I can hear the tiny footsteps of one of my three little angels heading toward me. I awaken to find one, two, or all three climbing and jumping on top of daddy while I painstakingly try to get rid of the cobwebs that have entered my sleepy head during the night.

To me, it is a wonderful experience. The most rewarding part of waking up in the morning is being brought out of semi-sleep (usually before 6 AM) by the sweet innocent sounds of my angels and being reminded that it's a new day. "Daddy, the sun is shining, wake up and make our breakfast," or, "Puleeease, Daddy, wake up, it's a new day, " is what I hear as I wake up. Am I still dreaming, or are these really my little angels waking me before most people start twisting and turning, subconsciously hoping that dreaded alarm clock malfunctions and doesn't go off?

Well, folks, there is no such luck here. No matter how many alarm clocks I chuck out the window like a Phil Simms bullet to Mark Bavaro, my three little angels will be sure to have their daddy up and ready to face a brand new day, usually way before even the moon starts going to sleep and the sun begins to wake up. To

Photo by Linda Kosarin

171

Field Judge:
Positions himself twenty-five yards downfield on tight end's side of field. Concentrates on tight end and defenders, looking for illegal blocks or holding infractions. Field judge also times intervals between plays and rules on deep holding or interference calls. Together with back judge, he rules on whether field goals and conversions are successful.

me, there is no better way to start a day. You'll never hear me complain because I know there will come a day (I hope I will live to see it) when "Daddy's Little Angels" will be all grown up, and I will yearn to hear their sweet little voices in my ear saying, "Wake up, Daddy! It's another beautiful day."

I guess what I'm saying is, live each day as if it's your last, because you never know if you're going to be around to reflect on and enjoy the past. Someday when I have the pleasure of meeting each and every one of you who purchased this book, you will see that this Pizza Dude will have a huge smile on his face and a kind word in his heart. I hope that through this book I have enriched you in some way, made some of you laugh, and provided you with a few tailgating tricks and wonderful recipes. But most of all I pray that I have brightened someone's day. It is for this reason that I awake each day to hear the voices of my sweet little angels telling me, "Good morning, Daddy. The sun is shinning and it's a brand new day!"

Drink and Be Merry

Photo by Seth Dinnerman

Photo by Seth Dinnerman

Drink and Be Merry

A good tailgate party strikes a natural balance of good friends, good food, the anticipation of a good game, and the availability of a wide assortment of beverages. The Pizza Man respects the right of everyone to enjoy the beverage of their choice, but I hope you will be smart enough to appoint a designated driver from your crew if your beverage of choice is alcoholic. Soft drinks, beer, wine, and bottled water are far and away the beverages of choice for tailgaters. When you are planning your tailgate, be sure to have a variety of beverages that will accommodate your crew and their guests. Always be sure to have a cooler and plenty of ice specifically for your beverages. Do not put drinks in the food cooler or use ice from it. You do not want to take a chance on some food-borne bacteria making its way into the ice cubes; it could ruin your day. Here is some fun information regarding beverages and their popularity, so relax, grab a cold one, and enjoy.

Coca-Cola

John Pemberton was born in Knoxville, Tennessee, in 1831. After attending pharmacy school, he operated a drug store in Columbus, Georgia. As a young man he fought for the Confederacy during the Civil War. He was wounded during the war and became addicted to morphine. After the war, Pemberton moved to Atlanta and started making and selling patent medicines. One of his biggest-selling items was French Wine of Coca.

It was a drink very similar to Vin Mariani, a Bordeaux wine, heavily laced with cocaine, that was immensely popular throughout the world. At the time, cocaine was not considered harmful, and doctors such as Sigmund Freud even touted its diverse uses. The formula for French Wine of Coca also contained caffeine from the kola nut.

Pemberton touted his concoction as a cure for nervous disorders, problems of internal plumbing, and impotency. In

Quarterback Pocket: In the 1930s and part of the 1940s, quarterbacks completed less than fifty percent of their passes because of ineffective blocking schemes on the offensive line. In the mid-1940s, legendary coach Paul Brown of the Cleveland Browns instituted an offensive line-blocking scheme that positioned the linemen in a "cup or pocketlike" blocking system. This unique blocking system changed the professional passing game forever.

**Giants No. 1
Draft Picks**

1970s

1970: Jim Files,
Oklahoma, LB
1971: Rocky
Thompson, West
Texas State, WR
1972: Eldridge Small,
Texas A & M, DB;
Larry Jacobson,
Nebraska, DE
1973: none
1974: John Hicks,
Ohio State, G
1975: none
1976: Troy Archer,
Colorado, DE
1977: Gary Jeter,
USC, DT
1978: Gordon King,
Stanford, T
1979: Phil Simms,
Morehead State, QB

November of 1885, bowing to Prohibitionist pressure, Atlanta voted to become a dry city as of July 1886.

Pemberton decided he would try a new marketing strategy by removing the wine and offering his product as a syrup-based medicine or fountain drink. Once the wine had been removed, the cocaine and caffeine that remained tasted very bitter. Over the next few months he began experimenting and added plenty of sugar to mask the bitterness. Citric acid was then added, providing some bite to balance the sweetness. Oils in various fruit flavors were also added to improve the taste. On May 8, 1886, in a laboratory in his house, Pemberton created the syrup that would later become Coca-Cola.

Pepsi-Cola

Pepsi-Cola shared similar roots with Coca-Cola in that the formulas were developed by men who owned or worked in pharmacies. Caleb D. Bradham of North Carolina left medical school in his second year because of financial hardship. Disappointed, but still possessing a love for medicine, Bradham bought a pharmacy in New Bern, North Carolina, in 1893, mostly on credit. The pharmacy contained a soda fountain, and young Caleb was good at creating his own flavored soft drinks. The drink he created and called Pepsi-Cola contained no cola and no caffeine, but it did taste similar to Coca-Cola, and Bradham wanted to capitalize on the popularity of Coca-Cola.

The Pepsi in the name comes from the ingredient pepsin, a digestive enzyme which was a popular ingredient in chewing gum. The drink proved to be wildly popular, and Bradham began wholesaling Pepsi syrup to other bottlers. By 1904, he began bottling it himself and also began selling Pepsi-Cola bottling franchises. By 1915, the Pepsi-Cola Corporation had assets in excess of $1 million. World War I proved to be the eventual downfall of the original Pepsi franchise. The cost of sugar, one of the primary ingredients, skyrocketed and brought the company to the verge of bankruptcy. In 1934, at the age of sixty-seven, Caleb Bradham died penniless, having been unable to hold on to his pharmacy.

7UP

In October of 1929, Charles Leiper Grigg invented a soft drink called Bib-Label Lithiated Lemon Lime Soda. Lithium, a lightweight metal now used in treating depression, was a popular ingredient in soft drinks of the time.

Needless to say, the original name didn't make it and was changed to 7UP in 1936. Why the name 7UP? No one seems to know for sure, but here are some thoughts:

There were, or are, seven ingredients in 7UP.

The original bottle was seven ounces.

It was named after a popular card game.

Mountain Dew

Mountain Dew was similar in taste to 7UP and was marketed as a mixer for bar drinks in the 1940s. It was also a lithiated lemon and lime drink and was named after the slang term for moonshine, the high-alcohol-content homemade liquor from the Appalachian hills. In 1964, Mountain Dew was acquired by Pepsi-Cola and has remained one of Pepsi's most popular brands.

Dr Pepper

In 1885, Charles Alderton, a pharmacist in Waco, Texas, was experimenting with different flavors for a cola-type soft drink, and is credited with inventing the formula that would become Dr Pepper. However, a Mr. Morrison, the owner of the drugstore, named the new soft drink. Morrison had worked for a Dr. Charles Pepper, and probably chose the name Dr Pepper because it was a way of paying tribute to the first person to give him a job. It was also a rather common practice to include "Dr." in a drink or product name (the period was dropped from Dr Pepper in the 1950s).

It was not long before other drugstore owners started buying the syrup from Alderton and Morrison, and the demand became so large that syrup sales were producing more profit

1980s

1980: Mark Haynes, Colorado, DB
1981: Lawrence Taylor, North Carolina, LB
1982: Butch Woolfork, Michigan, RB
1983: Terry Kinard, Clemson, DB
1984: Carl Banks, Michigan State, LB; William Roberts, Ohio State, T
1985: George Adams, Kentucky, RB
1986: Eric Dorsey, Notre Dame, DE
1987: Mark Ingram, Michigan State, WR
1988: Eric Moore, Indiana, T
1989: Brian Williams, Minnesota, C-G

than the rest of the drugstore. Morrison found a solution to this problem by bottling Dr Pepper.

Dr Pepper's major promotional opportunity came in 1904 at the World's Fair Exposition in St. Louis. This was the same World's Fair that saw the introduction of the ice cream cone and hamburgers and hot dogs served on buns. Nearly twenty million people attended the World's Fair and sampled Dr Pepper for the first time.

Dr Pepper's most intriguing marketing gimmick centered around the numbers "10, 2, 4" on the bottle cap. In 1927, the company asked Dr. Walter H. Eddy of Columbia University to conduct a study to determine the times of day when people felt fatigued. The doctor found that there was an energy drop at 10:30 AM, 2:30 PM, and 4:30 PM. The results of the study implied that if you wanted to avoid fatigue, you should drink Dr Pepper at 10, 2, and 4.

Beer

No one actually knows when beer was first brewed. The oldest records of brewing beer date back more than six thousand years to the ancient Sumerians. The land of Sumer was between the Tigris and Euphrates rivers, near southern Mesopotamia. The good folks discovered the fermentation process by sheer luck. The most plausible scenario for the discovery seems to be that a

Photo by Seth Dinnerman

piece of bread became wet and was left to lie around, forgotten. After some time, the bread began to ferment, and a pulp resulted. When the pulp was mixed with water and drunk, a nice buzz followed. The Sumerians were able to refine this process and are considered to be the first civilized culture to brew beer. They had discovered a "divine drink," which they offered to their gods. I wonder what their thoughts would be today about a $5.50 cost for a beer at the stadium?

Top Ten Best-Selling Soft Drinks

1. Coca-Cola Classic
2. Pepsi-Cola
3. Diet Coke
4. Mountain Dew
5. Sprite
6. Dr Pepper
7. Diet Pepsi
8. 7UP
9. Caffeine Free Diet Coke
10. Caffeine Free Pepsi and Barq's Root Beer (Tied)

   Source: Beverage World

Top Ten Best-Selling Beers

1. Budweiser
2. Bud Light
3. Miller Light
4. Coors Light
5. Busch
6. Natural Light
7. Miller Genuine Draft
8. Miller High Life
9. Busch Light Draft
10. Old Milwaukee

   Source: Beverage World

1990s

1990: Rodney Hampton, Georgia, RB
1991: Jarrod Bunch, Michigan, RB
1992: Derek Brown, Notre Dame, TE
1993: none
1994: Thomas Lewis, Indiana, WR
1995: Tyrone Wheatley, Michigan, RB
1996: Cedric Jones, Oklahoma, DE
1997: Ike Hilliard, Florida, WR
1998: Shaun Williams, UCLA, DB
1999: Luke Petitgout, Notre Dame, OT

Thirst Quencher

The Pizza Man's Fruit Sangria

A loaf of bread, a jug of wine, and 78,000 screaming Giants fans, and you have the makings of a good tailgate party. Wine making, like beer brewing, goes way back into antiquity. Can you imagine the rush the first guy had when he drank the fermented juice of grapes and started feeling that happy glow? All the Pizza Man has to say to that guy is thanks and God bless!

The Pizza Man's recipe for fruit sangria will lift your spirits regardless of the team's record.

> *2 sliced red apples*
> *1 cup seedless white grapes*
> *3 ripe peaches, sliced*
> *1 gallon red wine*

At least two hours before game time put fruit in punch bowl and add wine. Allow to stand for a while and enjoy.

Players & Fans

New Jersey
GIANTS6
Garden State

Photo by Seth Dinnerman

RALPH DEBBIE — OWNED & OPERATED BY GIANTS FANS — RUSS JUDY

GIANTS

BH·291P

Photo by Seth Dinnerman

Rocky! Rocky! Rocky!

This story is about one of our many questionable number-one draft picks, a player who didn't quite fit the description of a New York Giant. I can only guess that upper management was finally trying to change their old-fashioned ways when they drafted him in the first round. As you know by the miserable results of those lean seventies, trying is always harder than achieving.

Nevertheless, in 1971 we drafted one of the most colorful players ever to don our beloved blue. I say colorful because the talent and flair he had for running with the football outshone what little ability he had for learning the playbook.

I remember one of the very first times he touched the ball as a New York Giant. He took it all the way for a touchdown, a move that could not have been scripted better, even by me. I think it might have been the third game of his career. We were playing in St. Louis against the Cardinals. I remember the enthusiasm and expectations we Giants fans had for this heralded rookie out of West Texas State University.

The media was telling us in every article how great this kid was going to be. In training camp, they said he was ahead of everyone. No one could catch him when the ball was in his hands.

So what does this guy do? In either his first or third game as a Giant, he takes the opening kickoff almost ninety yards for a touchdown. I remember this vividly. I was a ten-year-old kid, so, of course, I was busy playing outside during the start of the game. I can still hear my dad screaming at the top of his lungs, "Go, Go, Go, Go, Go, Go, Go, Go, Go, TOUCHDOWN!" Well, not

Photo by Seth Dinnerman

183

only did my friends and I know that the Giants scored, but I think half of Bensonhurst knew as well. All the hype about this player who was going to save our sorry-assed franchise looked as though it would come true.

As we all know now, this was not to be. The seventies turned out to be extremely lean years to say the least. He did, however, give us tortured fans some hope, though it was false hope. I do have to admit, though, it was a lot of fun watching this guy run with the football. The funniest thing was watching the coaches go crazy while trying to draw the plays for him with a stick on the infield dirt at Yankee Stadium. I told you he could run, but think? I don't think so.

In those days the chants you heard booming from the rafters of Yankee Stadium were not just "Dee-fense, Dee-fense!" but also "ROCKY! ROCKY!" Rocky Thompson was fast becoming a threat to the rest of the league. Unfortunately, they quickly found a way to stop him; they just didn't kick him the football. This resulted in the ultimate demise of the original Rocky. The chant that we in New York had started was becoming a whisper. Some ten years later, another brainless, underdog hero arrived on our movie screens out of the streets

of Philadelphia, and suddenly all of America was using our chant, "ROCKY! ROCKY!" Isn't it just like Philadelphia fans to be ten years behind the times? Every so often while I am setting up for my Monster Tailgate Parties, when the parking lot is relatively quiet and the wind is blowing just right, I swear I can still hear it ever so faintly—Rocky! Rocky! Rocky!

Heard Around the Locker Room

I have been fortunate, in my association with Big Blue Travel, to visit most of the stadiums in the NFC and the AFC while my beloved Giants are on the road. When it comes to evaluating fans around the league, the Pizza Man has tried to maintain some objectivity. Being born into a family with several generations of Giants season-ticket holders has made this task difficult. Sure, some teams have fans that are as loud and crazy as Giants fans, but in my humble opinion they lack the primary traits that separate Giants fans from the rest of the pack: loyalty under the most adverse situations, an incredible degree of sophistication about the game, and a willingness to support a team through good and bad times. As a longtime Giants fan, I always wondered what the players on the field thought of the fans in the stands while the games were being played. While putting this book together, I had an opportunity to ask Giants coaches and players, past and present, what they thought of Giants fans, where the toughest places are in the league to play, and who their heroes were when they were growing up. Here are their comments.

Head Coach Jim Fassel—Fifteenth head coach in team history. Hired on January 15, 1997. Led the Giants in his first year to a 10–5–1 record, a playoff berth, and captured the NFC East Championship. Also named NFL Coach of the Year.

On Giants fans:

They're great fans. I have never seen fans as emotional about their team. You can see it when they talk about their team. It's done with such passion and feeling. When you're winning, there is no louder and more appreciative place to play than Giants Stadium. When you're losing, man, can they boo. The reason for that is because of their loyalty and knowledge of the game. They're very emotional.

Where is/was the toughest place to play?
Kansas City and Denver.

Photo by Linda Kosarin

185

Your favorite player/athlete while growing up?

I admired the guy right through high school and college—Joe "Willie" Namath.

What is the most memorable game you have ever been involved in?

Beating Washington in 1997 to clinch the NFC East title. This game stands out because I don't ever remember being as nervous or jittery before a game.

Photo by Jim Turner

Lawrence Taylor—(LB) North Carolina University. Number two draft pick in 1981. With Giants from 1981 to 1994. Only pro player to appear in ten consecutive Pro Bowls. Voted the NFL's MVP in 1986, the first defensive player to win since 1971. Led Giants to two Super Bowl victories. Finished career with 142 sacks, among the all-time leaders. On October 10, 1994, his No. 56 jersey was retired by the Giants. On January 30, 1999, he was elected to the Pro Football Hall of Fame on a first ballot in his first year of eligibility. He was certainly the greatest player I have ever seen. Born February 4, 1959.

On Giants fans:

They are the best! Without them there wouldn't be sports. We need their support and enthusiasm in the stands. When I was playing football, having them there and cheering us on meant the world to me. Still, to this day, it's great when I go to appearances or autograph sessions—the attendance is enormous. And when I get fan mail and the fans show they care and are still behind me, it really hits home. I think Giants fans are the best!

Where is/was the toughest place to play?

Tiger Stadium; Death Valley; Clemson, South Carolina.

Your favorite player/athlete while growing up?

Julius Erving (Dr. J) and Muhammad Ali.

What is the most memorable game you have ever been involved in?

Washington Redskins at Washington in 1986.

Charles Way—(FB) Virginia. Drafted in the sixth round (206th pick overall). With Giants from 1995 to present. A bruising

186

fullback who punishes defenders. Charles has stepped into a leadership role on the team, and has brought new energy to the offense. Born December 27, 1972.

Photo by Jim Turner

On Giants fans:
Great when you win, tough when you lose.

Where is/was the toughest place to play?
Kansas City.

Your favorite player/athlete while growing up?
Wilbert Montgomery.

What is the most memorable game you have ever been involved in?
My first college game against Wake Forest. I scored two touchdowns.

Kent Graham—(QB) Ohio State. Drafted in the eighth round (211th pick overall). With Giants from 1992 to 1994; waived on August 30, 1995; re-signed as a free agent on February 17, 1998. After taking over from Dave Brown in the middle of the season, Kent's leadership and a 5–1 performance helped turn a difficult season into a respectable 8–8. Kent reports to this year's camp as the incumbent starter at quarterback. Born November 1, 1968.

Photo by Jim Turner

On Giants fans:
The most educated and loyal fans in the NFL. They are the best.

Where is/was the toughest place to play?
Giants Stadium.

Your favorite player/athlete while growing up?
Walter Payton.

What is the most memorable game you have ever been involved in?
Last year's Denver game when we upset them to end their consecutive game-winning streak. It was great to beat a contender.

Phil McConkey—(WR) Navy. With Giants from 1984 to 1988. A fearless, intelligent player with great, soft hands. Phil had a knack for being in the right place at the right time. He probably

Photo by Jim Turner

is best remembered for his clutch catch of a touchdown pass that bounced off Mark Bavaro in the end zone, propelling the Giants to their Super Bowl win. Born February 24, 1957.

On Giants fans:

They show up. I can remember in 1989 we played in Dallas and 26,000 fans showed up. Giants fans show up no matter how the season is going or the team's record.

Where is/was the toughest place to play?

"Always Windy," Chicago Stadium.

Your favorite player/athlete while growing up?

O. J. Simpson.

What is the most memorable game you have ever been involved in?

The Giants' first Super Bowl win.

Chris Calloway—(WR) Michigan. Drafted in the fourth round by the Pittsburgh Steelers (97th pick overall). Signed by the Giants from the Steelers on March 31, 1992, as a Plan B free agent. With Giants from 1992 to present. Became a starter in 1993 after Mike Sherrard was hurt, and has not lost his starting position since. Born March 29, 1968.

On Giants fans:

Pretty loyal. They come out every Sunday, win or lose. Very tough when you lose, but still support you every step of the way.

Where is/was the toughest place to play?

In college at Wisconsin. Very rowdy fans. I guess 'cause they get all liquored up.

Your favorite player/athlete while growing up?

Michael Jordan.

What is the most memorable game you have ever been involved in?

College: I was a junior at Michigan in 1989, and we beat USC in the Rose Bowl. I scored a touchdown.

Pro: When we beat the Detroit Lions in OT in 1997.

Tiki Barber—(RB) Virginia. Drafted in second round in 1997 (36th pick overall). With Giants from 1997 to present. Began his rookie season as a starting running back after beating out Tyrone Wheatley in the preseason. Has identical twin brother, Rhonde. They played football together their whole lives, right through college at Virginia, but were separated when they became pros (Rhonde was drafted by the Tampa Bay Buccaneers). Born April 7, 1975.

Photo by Jim Turner

On Giants fans:
They can be brutal, but they're always there.

Where is/was the toughest place to play?
Tallahassee—Florida State. Very noisy and intimidating.

Your favorite player/athlete while growing up?
Walter Payton.

What is the most memorable game you have ever been involved in?
Thursday night, November 4, 1995, against Florida State on national TV. It was the first time they lost to an ACC Conference Team. It was my breakout game. I had 311 all-purpose yards, 193 yards receiving, with 2 touchdowns.

Eric Dorsey—(DE) Notre Dame University. A number one draft choice in 1986. With Giants from 1986 to 1992. Also a big contributer to both Super Bowl victories. Born August 5, 1964.

Photo by Jim Turner

On Giants fans:
They are great. Very loyal.

Where is/was the toughest place to play?
Philly. Their fans and field are the worst in the NFL.

Your favorite player/athlete while growing up?
I really didn't have a favorite player.

What is the most memorable game you have ever been involved in?
When we beat the Redskins in the 1986 NFC Championship Game on January 11, 1987.

Photo by Jim Turner

Stacey Robinson—(WR) North Dakota State. A number two draft pick in 1985. With Giants from 1985 to 1988. In my opinion, one of if not the best clutch receivers the Giants have ever had. A major contributor to both Super Bowl victories. Born February 19, 1962.

On Giants fans:
They are truly the greatest fans there are. I love 'em! Extremely knowledgeable. Unlike any other fans. New York fans are a breed apart.

Where is/was the toughest place to play?
Philly. Horrendous field.

Your favorite player/athlete while growing up?
Other than Mom? Paul Warfield.

What is the most memorable game you have ever been involved in?
Super Bowl XXI, January 25, 1986. Pasadena Rose Bowl. 39–20 victory over the Denver Broncos.

Photo by Jim Turner

Sean Landeta—(P) Towson State University. With Giants from 1985 to 1993. His amazing ability to kick booming punts with long hang times was an integral part of the Giants' successful Super Bowl seasons. Sean has been a longtime favorite of Giants fans, and I have never seen him refuse a request for an autograph. Born January 6, 1962.

On Giants fans:
Giants fans are some of the most passionate and knowledgeable fans in the whole country. They really live for their team.

Where is/was the toughest place to play?
Anywhere on the road in the NFL.

Your favorite player/athlete while growing up?
My dad.

What is the most memorable game you have ever been involved in?
Two games—Super Bowl XXI and Super Bowl XXV.

Howard Cross—(TE) Alabama. Drafted in sixth round in 1989. With Giants from 1989 to present. A fierce blocker with good hands, Howard is a vital part of the Giants offense. Also one of the better blocking tight ends in the NFL, and his receiving abilties have improved every year. A real "gamer," his streak of 103 straight games played was broken when he underwent microscopic surgery on his knee. In 1995, he was named by the Giants as the True Value Man of the Year for his tireless community work. Born August 8, 1967.

Photo by Jim Turner

On Giants fans:

They do a great job. Extremely loyal. They are not always happy, but that is usually our fault. They are true and great fans.

Where is/was the toughest place to play?

Philadelphia. The turf was terrible. It hurt to run on it, walk on it, or just plain stand on it.

Your favorite player/athlete while growing up?

"Dr. J," Julius Erving.

What is the most memorable game you have ever been involved in?

Alabama vs. Auburn in my first year of college. Back then they used to divide the stadium right down the middle. On one side of the stadium sat 40,000 Alabama fans. On the other side, 40,000 Auburn fans. It was quite an event.

Brian Williams—(C) Minnesota. Drafted in first round in 1989 (18th pick). With Giants from 1989 to present. Was on the verge of becoming one of the best centers in the league when a freak eye injury in training camp in 1998 almost ended his career. Plans to return in 1999. Born June 8, 1966.

Photo by Jim Turner

On Giants fans:

No question, the most loyal fans there are. The Giants have been sold out forever and probably always will.

Where is/was the toughest place to play?

Texas Stadium.

Your favorite player/athlete while growing up?
Terry Bradshaw. I grew up in Pittsburgh.

What is the most memorable game you have ever been involved in?
Has to be the 1990 Super Bowl.

Jason Sehorn—(CB) USC. Drafted in second round in 1994. With Giants from 1994 to present. Jason is fast becoming one of the elite defensive players in the NFL. His athletic ability and pure instinct are unparalleled. After missing the entire 1998 season with a devastating knee injury, I am sure Jason will be back in 1999, stronger and better than ever. Born April 15, 1976.

On Giants fans:
They are the best. Very loyal. No matter what, they show up. They may not be there to cheer you all the time and that's OK. We probably deserve it. Rest assured they are always there.

Where is/was the toughest place to play?
Penn State University. Getting there was a horror. There is no airport for miles and miles. You have to drive a long way to get there. Then you have to play in front of 97,000 hostile fans.

Your favorite player/athlete while growing up?
Athlete—Nolan Ryan. Person—Mom.

What is the most memorable game you have ever been involved in?
1998 Minnesota playoff game. Although we lost, it was an epic battle.

Phillippi Sparks—(CB) Arizona State. Drafted in second round by the Giants in 1992 (41st pick overall). With Giants from 1992 to present. Loves physical play and has been a starter since the 1993 season. Has established himself as one of the top cornerbacks in the NFL. Born April 15, 1969.

On Giants fans:
The most loyal fans there are! They say fans in Cleveland and the "dog pound" are loyal, but nothing compares to a Giants fan!

Where is/was the toughest place to play?
In college, against the Washington Huskies, because of their fans. And it's real cold!

Your favorite player/athlete while growing up?
"Dr. J," Julius Erving.

What is the most memorable game you have ever been involved in?
When we won the National Junior College Championship at Glendale CC in Arizona.

Editor's Note:
While working with the Pizza Man for the last year, I had an opportunity to speak with some of the players that Willie had interviewed. I asked the same players and coaches what their thoughts were about the Pizza Man as a fan. Here are some of their comments:

Coach Fassel
Outstanding! Represents all that there is to represent. He's always dressed in blue, even on the road. He's the greatest and most dedicated fan I know. My players should have the heart and desire he brings to the games, it would make my job a lot easier.

Lawrence Taylor
When I think of the Pizza Man, an Italian kid from Brooklyn, three things come to mind:

One, the truest Giants fan I've ever seen. Two, in the eighties, you could always depend on the Pizza Man being at every game. Three, not only a Giants fan but a Giants friend!

Charles Way
The most loyal fan I know.

Kent Graham
He's great for the team, never shy to voice his opinion.

Giants Fan Sites on the Internet

The following listing of Giants-related sites on the internet represents only a small portion of those sites that are available.

Any of these sites will help you navigate to other links that you may want to explore.

Giants: The official Giants site with loads of team related info, www.giants.com

NFL: The official site of the NFL. All teams, including the Giants, can be linked through this site at www.nfl.com

NFL fans: A really good site to learn more about the rules and regulations of the game. This site is also full of interesting historical facts and stories about the development of the game we know today, www.NFL.fan.com

Big Blue Travel: The official road-trip company of the Football Giants. Five-star mini-vacations at only the best hotels each opponent's city has to offer. A real first-class operation. Check it out at www.giantsroad-trips.com

Big Blue Wrecking Crew: A great interactive site for dedicated Big Blue fans. Check it out at www.bbwc.com

Broadcasts: Get post-game as well as Monday and Wednesday live press conference broadcasts by Giants Head Coach Jim Fassel at www.broadcast.com

Inside football: An informative site that has a special listing of restaurants and sports bars around the country that broadcast Giants games via satellite, www.insidefootball.com

Phil McConkey
Top of the list, as far as fans go. Always seen and heard. He gets under the skin of the opposing team, and it's great to see and hear him do that because we get it on the road. I think he's been there since the stadium has been there.

Chris Calloway
The ultimate fan. True Blue—always there, no matter what.

Tiki Barber
Biggest fan I know, always there. Pizza Man is everywhere!

Stacy Robinson
Typical. I say typical only because I think very highly of Giants fans. Therefore, the Pizza Man is typical. Like all the rest, loyal and very passionate.

Sean Landeta
Impossible to find a bigger fan. There may be one equal, but none bigger than the Pizza Man.

Howard Cross
He's great. The biggest supporter I have ever seen. More fans should be like the Pizza Man. He's the best there is, a great guy, and equally great for the team.

Brian Williams
The most loyal fan. There are a handful of guys above the tunnel we recognize all the time. Pizza Man sort of sticks out of the crowd, though. He's great for the team. Always tries to get us pumped up.

Jason Sehorn
Entertaining, to say the least. He's always there and lets you know it. Everyone on the field has a different story about how he became known as the Pizza Man.

Phillippi Sparks
Pizza Man, you're the man!

Wrap Up the Season and Take It Home

On Sunday, February 7, 1999, the same day the NFL Pro Bowl was played in sunny Hawaii, Big Blue Travel held their Eighth Annual New York Giants Wrap-Up Breakfast at the equally exotic Sheraton Plaza Hotel in East Rutherford, New Jersey.

I can tell you this, folks, it was the most enjoyable event that I've had the pleasure to attend. The guest list at this event brought together players whose talent, love, and desire to play football was unequaled during their playing time with the Giants. The enthusiasm and affection that these players felt for the more than six hundred die-hard Giants fans in attendance was genuine.

For the Giants fans who were there, you witnessed one of the most memorable events in recent team history. In one huge ballroom, there were retired players destined for the Pro Football Hall of Fame alongside current veterans and rookies who dream of being in that same Pro Football Hall of Fame some day.

The top billing went to three of the greatest running backs in the seventy-five-year history of the New York Football Giants. First there was Joe Morris, a product of Syracuse University, one of the players who carried us all the way to our first Super Bowl appearance and victory.

Then we were humbled by the appearance of a product of the University of Georgia, a man who also carried our team most of his career, a man who never stopped trying for those extra yards, and who holds the New York Giants record (among others) for the most consecutive one-thousand-yard rushing seasons—none other than Rodney Hampton.

Finally we came to the elder statesman of the three. The rare athlete who not only can take over a football game, but—like me—can take over a roomful of people as well, a guy who earned the reputation of a workhorse who never quit, who

Mike Francesa's New York Sports: Mike is the co-host of the popular Mike and the Mad Dog show on radio WFAN 660 FM in New York. Mike is also featured on Game Day Live on CBS. Francesa is one of the very best at what he does, and if anyone is on top of the New York sports scene, it's big Mike. Check it out at www.mikesports.com

Brooksie's NY Giants Site: A fan-friendly interactive site that posts photos of Giants players and offers chat rooms, at www.pages.prodigy.net/brooksie/giants

Other sites of interest for Giants fans:

www.bergenrecord.com —The Bergen Record is Bergen County's largest circulation daily newspaper, with extensive coverage of the Giants. Check out the columns by Vinny DiTrani, the Giants beat writer and an award-winning journalist.

always kept his legs and heart churning, no matter what the obstacles; a product out of Miami University, who sports a Super Bowl ring on each hand and was the MVP of Super Bowl XXV—O. J. Anderson.

All you had to do was replace the football they usually carried with a microphone, and we had a wonderful opportunity to see and hear our heroes give something back to the fans. Between the laughter and the good-natured ribbing they gave each other, the crowd intently awaited every word they spoke. Each of them talked sincerely and passionately about the wonderful careers they enjoyed, the professionalism of the Giants organization, and more importantly, the most loyal, knowledgeable, and dedicated fans a team could ever hope for. On a personal note, O. J. Anderson gave me the most unforgettable and amazing honor a Giants fan could ever receive. I got to wear one of his rings. It was only for about ten minutes, but can you believe it? Me, little ol' Willie "The Pizza Man" Mariano, an Italian-American from Bensonhurst, Brooklyn, wearing a 1986 Super Bowl ring. It was one of the best ten minutes of my life, and I thank you, Mr. Ottis Jerome Anderson, from the bottom of my True-Blue heart.

Well, believe it or not, folks, besides these three unforgettable Giants, there were more. There was the soon-to-be-Hall of Famer out of South Carolina State University, eleven-year Pro Bowler, Mr. Harry Carson. Right next to him was the fan favorite and a guy with a heart as big as a whole fleet of battleships, out of the Naval Academy, Mr. Phil McConkey. While these were all leaders of past Giants teams, there were also guys there who lead our current team.

First was the leader of the whole bunch, the 1997 NFL Head Coach of the Year, the man who is doing an outstanding job and will continue to do so until he brings home that ultimate prize, the Lombardi Trophy, Mr. Jim Fassel.

In addition to Coach Fassel, there was the quiet and resilient product out of Virginia who led a committee of running backs through pretty large holes in 1997, Charles Way, and a host of others, including Percy Ellsworth, Derek Engler, Roman Oben,

Robert Massey, Mike Cherry, Greg Comella, and Pete Monty. There was one more guy I saved for last. He was chosen by Big Blue Travel as the "Man of the Year," a guy who was taken back by our head coach at the beginning of the 1998 season from the Arizona Cardinals as insurance for second-year quarterback Danny Kanell. This player seized an opportunity when it presented itself, took over a sinking team, and brought back the respect it so justly deserved. Just by using his experience and God-given abilities, Kent Graham became a leader for a team that was desperately in search of one. He started the last seven games of the season and went 6–1. By example, he taught the younger guys how to win.

This wonderful day ended for me on a special note. As I was thanking all the True-Blue fans who attended, I was met by a group of underprivileged youngsters who were brought to the breakfast as guests of the NFL Alumni Association, headed by Howie Carp, a former Giants water boy in 1959. These adorable kids (there had to be about forty of them), from ages three to fifteen, saw me alone and swarmed over to me for autographs. I asked them, "What happened, all the players left and you need to fill some space in your programs?" Their response was amazing: "You're the man, Pizza Dude," they screamed.

One sweet, innocent child shouted, "The players are just players, but you, you're the man, the Fan's Fan." Now, you might say, give me a break, the Pizza Man signing autographs? However, to me it was so sweet and touching the way they all swarmed around me as if I were a star they had come to see.

The one little girl who really got to me was Rose. She was such an angel and waited so patiently to get her autograph, and when she did, she gave me the biggest hug and kiss I have ever received and just stole my heart away. Her eyes were as bright as the clear blue sky and she simply said, "I love pizza!" Wow! Folks, I cannot begin to tell you how that felt. As a guy who always has time and energy for the kids, it just made me want to stop and acknowledge the precious gifts God put on this earth for us to guide and nourish—the children.

www.nj.com—The website of the *Newark Star-Ledger* has great coverage of the Giants.

www.profootballhof.com—This is the official site of the Pro Football Hall of Fame. Full of wonderful info and is, of course, rich in history.

www.ballparks.com—An informative site for everything you ever wanted to know about sports stadiums.

Fan Tribute

I don't think it's possible for a person to dream of a better six or seven years than I have had while pursuing this book project.

Besides thanking everyone who had a part in this project, I must thank my family in Blue, my fellow fans. You folks are very special to me. We have suffered together through the lean years and celebrated together through the championship years. This is why when I questioned players for this book about their feelings about Giants fans, every one of them said how loyal we are, how we always show up no matter what the record.

Well, they don't know the half of it. Being born New York Football Giants fans, we go far beyond what is expected of the average football fan. It's not just about football and backing up your team no matter what, it's about pride; it's about believing in your heart that there is nothing bad anyone can say about your team as long as you remain "True Blue." For some of us during the season, it is about reading every piece of information you can find in the papers and watching every highlight clip available on TV. During the off-season (a trying and depressing time for this Big Blue fan), it's about watching

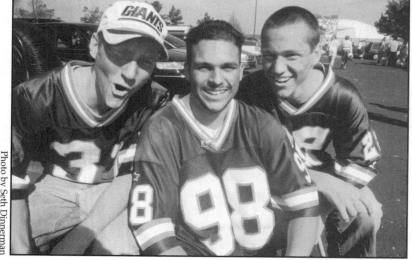

videotapes of games played the year before or even ten years before. It's about searching for the tiniest clip in the newspapers about our G-Men among page after page of boring articles on basketball, hockey, and golf.

You may say, "This guy has got to be kidding, there are so many more important things in life than Giants football, things like owning your

Photo by Seth Dinnerman

198

own home, being successful, being healthy, or even world peace." Don't get me wrong, folks, I am an adamant believer in all the good things life has to offer, and also in achieving the lofty goals we all set for ourselves, but tell me this: is any of it worth a hoot if you don't have Giants football in your life? I think not!

Photo by Seth Dinnerman

To me, life without Giants football would be like getting three aces in one round of golf while playing all by yourself. Who's going to believe you? Even worse, it would be like winning twenty-million dollars and not being able to spend it, like finding an angel in your closet and not being able to show anyone.

Like all of my True-Blue friends that I have made throughout the years at the Meadowlands and all over the country, I believe that there is no better place to be than at Giants Stadium—even in the dead of winter on a day when even penguins seek shelter—to watch our G-Men dismantle an opponent. Whether it is a patsy team like the Colts or a hated rival like the Cowboys, the feeling is always the same; it is a feeling of achievement and pride that cannot be equaled. Well, actually, it's a little better when we beat the Cowboys . . .

Official Hand Signals

Touchdown, field goal, or successful try

Ball illegally touched, kicked, or batted

False start, illegal formation, kickoff kick out of bounds, or kicking team player voluntarily out of bounds during a punt

Pass juggled inbounds and caught out of bounds

Safety

Time out

Personal foul

Illegal forward pass

First down

No time out or time in with wistle

Holding

Intentional grounding of pass

Reprinted with permission from NFL Properties.

Crowd noise, dead ball, or neutral zone established

Delay of game or excess time out

Illegal use of hands, arms, or body

Interference with forward pass or fair catch

Ineligible receiver or ineligible member of kicking team downfield

Interlocking interference, pushing, or helping runner

Penalty refused, incomplete pass, play over, or missed goal

Invalid fair catch signal

Illegal contact

Touching a forward pass or scrimmage kick

Player disqualified

Face mask

Offside, encroachment, or neutral zone infraction

Unsportsmanlike conduct

Tripping

Illegal shift

Illegal motion at snap

Illegal cut, illegal block below the waist, chop block, or clipping

Illegal substitution, 12 men in offense huddle, or too many men on the field

Reset play clock— 25 seconds

  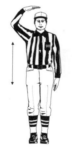 

Loss of down

Illegal crackback

Uncatchable forward pass

Reset play clock— 40 seconds

Pizza Man's Football Glossary

While you may consider yourself a true fan with no need for a glossary, keep in mind that some of your tailgate guests may not have the same feel for the game as you do. This glossary is provided for those new or casual fans who might need some help to enjoy the game.

Artificial Turf: A composite surface made from plastic. Used instead of natural grass in many football stadiums.

Audible: A change in the play call made at the line of scrimmage by the quarterback. The play is changed by a verbal command before the snap.

Backfield: The area behind the line of scrimmage.

Backs: Usually running backs, halfbacks, or fullbacks who line up with the quarterback in the backfield.

Ball Carrier: Any player who has possession of the ball during a play.

Blitz: An all-out rushing assault by the defense on the offensive line in an attempt to tackle the quarterback before he can make a play.

Blocking: When offensive players, using their arms and bodies, try to prevent the defensive players from tackling the ball carrier.

Bomb: A long pass play to a receiver running down the field.

Bump and Run: A technique used by a pass defender for the defensive team, occurring when he is allowed to make contact with a potential offensive pass receiver one time within ten yards of the line of scrimmage in order to slow the receiver down and prevent him from catching a pass thrown by the quarterback.

Clipping: An illegal block that hits an opponent below the waist from behind. It is considered a personal foul and results in a fifteen-yard penalty to the team committing the foul.

Completed Pass: When a player catches a forward pass while the ball is in the air.

Conferences: The groups into which teams are divided. The NFL is comprised of the National and American Conferences.

Control the Clock: Play strategy employed by the offensive team to either save or use up time on the game clock.

Coverage: The aim here is to "cover" or prevent a player from gaining yards. A pass defender "covers" a receiver to prevent him from catching a pass.

Cut Back: A controlled, quick change of direction by a ball carrier or pass receiver to elude a defender who is trying to tackle them.

Dead Ball: A ball is "dead" when a play has ended. The ball is "live" the moment the offensive center snaps the ball back to the quarterback.

Divisions: The categories within conferences into which teams are grouped, usually by geographical locations such as Eastern, Western, or Central Divisions.

Double Coverage: When two pass defenders cover one receiver.

Down: One of four chances the offensive team has to advance the ball ten yards. Also used to describe a ball carrier who has been tackled.

Draft Choice: A player chosen from a pool of college players by a football team. The college draft is an annual affair.

Drive: A series of successful plays that helps an offensive team move down the field in an attempt to score.

Drop Back: The quarterback takes the snap from the center and takes several steps backward in order to pass the ball downfield.

Eligible Receiver: A player who is allowed to catch a forward pass. Technically, all offensive players, with the exception of the linemen and the quarterback, are eligible receivers.

Encroachment: When a player, except the center who snaps the ball, is lined up in the "neutral zone" (the space between the offensive line and the defensive line) and contact occurs before the ball is snapped, a player has committed an encroachment foul and his team is penalized five yards.

End Line: The boundary line that runs across the width of the field at the far end of the end zone.

End Zone: An area that the offensive team attempts to enter in order to score a touchdown. It is the ten-yard-long area between the goal line and the end line and is bordered by the sidelines.

Extra Point(s): Additional point(s) scored by the offensive team after they have scored a touchdown. One point for kicking the ball through the goalposts and two points for passing or running the ball over the goal line.

Fair Catch: A player who is about to receive a kickoff or punt waves one hand in the air—the signal for "fair catch." After giving this signal, the player cannot be hit or tackled by the opposing team, and he cannot advance the ball.

Field Goal: A placekick that passes above the crossbar and between the upright portions of the goalpost. A successful kick is awarded three points.

Field Position: Where a team is located on the field in relation to the two goal lines. Good field position is when a team is close to the opponent's goal line; bad field position is when a team is close to its own goal line.

First Down: The first of four chances the offensive team has to advance the ball ten yards. When ten yards have been gained within the four downs, the offensive team earns a new first down and four more chances to advance the ball ten or more yards.

Forward Pass: A pass usually thrown by the quarterback toward the opponent's goal line. A forward pass can be thrown only from behind the line of scrimmage.

Forward Progress: The spot on the field where a ball carrier or receiver has advanced the ball and is stopped by the defense.

Foul: An illegal action by a team member that results in a penalty.

Franchise: The legal agreement between team owners and the NFL that allows the team to be a part of the NFL.

Free Agent: A player whose contract with a team has expired. The player is allowed to negotiate with other teams for his services.

Free Kick: A free kick is used to start play after a touchdown and extra point have occurred (kickoff), or when a safety has occurred. Defenders must line up at least ten yards away from the kicking team.

Fumble: When the ball carrier loses possession of the ball by dropping it or having it knocked from his grasp before a play ends. The player who regains possession of the loose ball is credited with a fumble recovery, and his team goes on offense.

Goal Line: A line across the width of the field ten yards from the end line that a player must cross to score a touchdown (six points).

Goalpost: The metal Y-shaped structure that stands at the back end of the end zone. Teams try to kick the ball above the crossbar and between the upright portions to score a field goal (three points) or an extra point (one point) after a touchdown.

Go For It: The offensive team is facing a fourth down and decides to try for a new first down instead of punting the ball. If the team fails to gain the necessary yardage for a first down, it loses possession of the ball, and the opponent then goes on offense from that spot on the field.

Handoff: A running play in which the quarterback takes the snap from the center and hands the ball off to a running back.

Hang Time: The amount of time a punted ball remains in the air.

Holding: When a player prevents the movement of another player by grabbing or holding on to any part of his body or uniform. Penalties for holding are ten yards, if committed by an offensive player (offensive team must then start from ten yards farther back); five yards (forward) plus a first down for the offensive team, if holding is committed by the defense.

Home Field Advantage: The alleged benefit derived by a team playing on their home field in front of their own fans and not having to travel to an opponent's field.

Home Game: A game played in the team's own stadium.

In Bounds: The legal playing area on the field inside the sidelines and end lines.

Intentional Grounding: When the quarterback purposely throws an incomplete forward pass into the ground in the backfield to avoid being sacked.

Interception: A pass intended for an offensive receiver that is caught by a defender. The defender's team then gains possession of the ball and goes on offense.

Kickoff: Used to start the game at the beginning of the second half and after each score. Ball is placed on a kicking tee and is kicked from the team's thirty-yard line toward the opposing team, who then tries to advance it.

Lateral: A pass thrown either laterally or backward to a teammate behind the line of scrimmage.

Line of Scrimmage: An imaginary line that no player may cross before the center snaps the ball to the quarterback. Each team has its own line of scrimmage, separated by the neutral zone.

Lineman: A player who starts each play positioned within one yard of his team's line of scrimmage.

Live Ball: A ball is considered live the moment the center snaps the ball back to the quarterback or the holder, if a kick is being attempted.

Loose Ball: A ball that is not in the possession of either team, such as after a fumble or a kickoff. A loose ball may be recovered by either team, and the team that recovers it goes on offense.

Man-in-Motion: A single offensive player who is permitted to move parallel to the line of scrimmage prior to the ball being snapped.

Midfield: The fifty-yard line that divides the two halves of the field.

Neutral Zone: The area between the offensive and defensive lines of scrimmage.

Nickel Defense: The defense brings in a fifth defensive back to replace a linebacker so they can have additional coverage against an attempted pass by the offense.

Offside: Occurs when any player, offensive or defensive, is beyond his line of scrimmage before the ball is snapped. Results in a five-yard penalty to the team that is offside.

Open Receiver: A player who has no defender closely covering him.

Out of Bounds: Areas of the field outside of the sidelines or end lines. When a ball carrier or the ball itself touches an out-of-bounds line, the play is immediately over.

Pass Defender: A defensive player who covers an opposition receiver.

Pass Patterns/Pass Routes: Predetermined paths receivers follow so the quarterback can anticipate where to throw the ball.

Pass Protection: Blocking by the offensive line, which tries to keep the defenders away from the quarterback so he can complete a pass.

Pass Rush: When defensive players attempt to get past blockers and sack (tackle in the backfield) the quarterback.

Personal Foul: A foul that may cause injury to an opposing player. Fifteen-yard penalties are given for personal fouls.

Picked Off: When an offensive forward pass is intercepted by a defender.

Place Kick: A kicking attempt for a field goal (three points) or an extra point (one point after a touchdown). The ball is snapped from center to a holder who places the ball on the ground, point down, and holds it with his fingers. Kicker then kicks the held ball.

Play: A prearranged action that begins with the snap of the ball.

Play Clock: A forty-second clock displayed above each end zone. Team has only forty seconds to initiate play by snapping ball. A delay-of-game penalty is assessed if play does not commence within the allotted forty seconds.

Play-Action Pass: Quarterback fakes a handoff to a running back in order to "freeze" the defenders so that he may attempt a forward pass.

Playoffs: A post-season tournament that eventually determines the NFL Champions.

Pass Pocket: The cup-like area formed by the offensive line where the quarterback is protected while he attempts a forward pass.

Point After Touchdown (PAT): An opportunity to placekick an extra point from the opponent's two-yard line after a touchdown has been scored.

Possession: To be holding or in control of the ball.

Previous Spot: The last position on the field from which the ball was snapped to begin the last play.

Punt: The punter stands ten yards behind the line of scrimmage, receives a snap from the center, drops it toward his kicking foot from approximately shoulder height, and before it makes contact with the ground, kicks the ball toward the opposing team, who then tries to catch and return the punt the other way.

Quarterback: The "field general" and leader of the offensive team. Communicates each play to his team in the huddle. Takes the snap from center and either hands off the ball to a running back, throws a forward pass to a receiver downfield, or runs with the ball himself.

Reading the Defense: The action by which the quarterback recognizes the defensive formations and anticipates the best type of play to execute. Usually a play is called in the huddle; however, if the quarterback recognizes a defensive formation he feels he might be able to exploit with a different play, he can then call an audible which will change the play that was called in the huddle.

Receiver: An offensive player who attempts to catch a forward pass.

Recovery: To gain or regain possession of the football after a fumble.

Return: An attempt by a player who has made an interception or caught a punt or kickoff to advance the ball toward the opponent's goal line.

Rollout: Occurs when a quarterback runs parallel to the line of scrimmage in an attempt to find a receiver downfield rather than throwing from the pocket. Rollout passes help spread the defense out as they pursue the quarterback, and the receiver may find out that he has less coverage.

Rookie: A first-year player in the NFL.

Sack: Occurs when the quarterback is tackled by the defense behind the line of scrimmage while he is in possession of the ball.

Safety: Occurs when a ball carrier is tackled in his own end zone by the defense. The defense is awarded two points and a free kick from the offense, who kick from their own twenty-yard line.

Scrambling: Evasive action by a quarterback to avoid being sacked by the defense.

Series: The four downs a team has to advance the ball ten or more yards for another first down.

Sideline: The boundary lines that run the length of the field on each side. If the ball carrier or the ball touch or cross these lines they are "out of bounds," and the play stops.

Snap: When the offensive center, facing forward toward the defensive line, snaps the ball through his legs to the quarterback standing behind him. The snap is the action that starts each play.

Special Teams: Players who participate in kicking plays.

Spike the Ball: When a player throws the ball to the ground after scoring a touchdown.

Spot: Where the official places the ball after a play to mark the forward progress of the play.

Stiff Arm: A technique used by a ball carrier to ward off a defender by pushing him out of the way with his stiff free arm.

Super Bowl: The final game of the playoffs. Determines the champion of the NFL. The game is played by NFC and AFC champions at a neutral site each January.

Tackle: A player position on the offensive and defensive lines. There is usually a left and right tackle on each line.

Tackling: The action used by a defender to bring a ball carrier to the ground and stop his forward progress.

Touchback: A touchback occurs when a player gains possession of a ball kicked into his end zone by the opponent, and then kneels on one knee. After a touchback, the next offensive play starts at the twenty-yard line. A touchback is also awarded when an opponent kicks the ball over the end line and out of the end zone.

Touchdown (TD): Occurs when a team crosses the opponent's goal line via a run or catch, or recovers a loose ball in the opponent's end zone. A touchdown is worth six points.

Turnover: An involuntary loss of possession of the ball during a play by a fumble or interception.

Two-Point Conversion: Occurs when a team that has just scored a touchdown chooses not to kick and tries to cross the goal line with a run or pass play. If successful, the team is awarded two points instead of one point for a kick.

Wild Card: A team that makes the playoffs by having one of the three best records among non-division winners within its conference.

Photo by Al Pereira

Hey Tailgating Fans!

Want to see your favorite tailgate recipe, photo, or story appear in print, and win a prize?

Send your favorite photos, recipes, stories, and your weekly tailgate location to:

Willie "The Pizza Man" Mariano
Columbus Circle Station
PO Box 20292
New York, NY 10023

Or visit us at www.pizzaman.com

Sometime during the season we will visit you at your tailgating location to talk about how you make your tailgate parties special.

If your photo, recipe, or story is selected, it will appear in our next edition of *Fan Feast*, and you will be automatically entered in a drawing to win a prize. Prizes will include "Pizza Man's Tailgate Crew" T-shirts for weekly winners and two tickets to a Big Blue Travel Giants fan event for our grand prize tailgate winner.

Please include your name, address, phone number, and primary tailgate location (if applicable).

Any materials sent cannot be returned and all selections and decisions by our panel of judges are final.